BEER HIKING QUEBEC

30 HIKES AND BREWERIES FROM MONTREAL TO THE GASPÉ PENINSULA

Beer Hiking Quebec
30 Hikes and Breweries from Montreal to the Gaspé Peninsula

By: Bianca Pomerleau

ISBN: 978-3-03964-080-5
Originally published in French as *Randos Bière au Québec*
Translated by Jeffrey K. Butt
Published by Helvetiq, Lausanne/Basel, Switzerland
Graphic Design and illustration: Elżbieta Kownacka
Printed in China
First Edition April 2025

info@helvetiq.ch

www.helvetiq.com/us
www.facebook.com/helvetiq_usa
instagram: @helvetiq_usa

helvetiq.com

BEER HIKING QUEBEC

30 HIKES AND BREWERIES FROM MONTREAL TO THE GASPÉ PENINSULA

BY BIANCA POMERLEAU
TRANSLATED BY JEFFREY K. BUTT

TABLE OF CONTENTS

1

INTRODUCTION

A WORD FROM THE AUTHOR

Hello! I'm Bianca. I'm a writer-editor, former music teacher, mother, and eternal student. I live in beautiful Quebec City, but I grew up in the region of Chaudière-Appalaches. As a traveler, avid hiker, serious craft beer enthusiast, and hard-core road tripper, I hide out behind a blog named *la Grande Déroute* (lagrandederoute.com), where I've been chronicling my global escapades since 2005. I'm also the author of this book: *Beer Hiking Quebec*. So nice to meet you!

My interest in all things beer dates back to 2002 when I participated in a beer-tasting workshop organized as part of a youth tourism conference. At the time, traveling was already a huge part of my life, but a trip to Belgium quickly sparked my interest in beer tourism. Ever since then, beer naturally finds a place in all my adventures. As for my love of hiking, well that developed gradually during my globe-trotting, and in recent years hiking has become a fixture in my life.

In April 2019 I discovered the Beer Hiking series during a press tour on the Opal Coast, organized for the launch of *Beer Hiking in France*. I immediately fell in love with the theme, which quickly became an obsession.

By the end of June 2019, after some back-and-forth with the Swiss-based publisher Helvetiq, I was off on an incredible, five-month road trip across Quebec. My mission: to discover microbreweries and hiking trails. My family tagged along for the initial two months. After that, I explored my *belle province* (beautiful province) either solo or with friends in tow.

This was the tally (and for just those five months): no less than 20,000 km placed on the odometer, 484 km of trails hiked, 54 microbreweries visited, and 403 new beers tasted. I can honestly say that Quebec lacks neither good beer nor spectacular scenery!

For the English edition of the book in 2025, I selected the 30 hikes and breweries best suited to locals as well as visitors from around the globe, and updated some beers and breweries that had changed.

It is my sincere wish that the itineraries chosen for this book inspire you to explore Quebec's magnificent regions, to make the most of its extraordinary natural environments, and to get out and meet those passionate brewers who make the province's brew scene what it is: diverse, delicious, and vibrant.

On that note, happy trails and enjoy the beer!

BEER HIKING IN QUEBEC: WHY?

Quebec's microbrew industry, a scene brimming with boldness and passion if ever there was one, is booming. In 2002, barely 30 licenses were issued (brewers and microbrewers combined). By the time I finished putting this book together, that number had risen to almost 250, and there's every reason to believe there's more growth to come[1].

Craft brews are products that truly reflect a region's identity. They're a tribute to its folklore, geography, wildlife, vegetation, residents, and history. As drivers of the food and beer tourism industry, breweries and their tasting rooms have become gathering places for locals and visitors alike. Need proof? Look no further than the many beer routes launched over the past few years.

At the same time, if there is truly one thing that sets this beautiful, vast province apart, it has to be its wide, open, larger-than-life spaces. Is there any other more wondrous way to explore Quebec's mountains, forests, and arctic landscapes than on foot? The thousands of miles of these trails don't even put a dent in what there is to see!

And after all that hard work, there's a chance to unwind. What a great idea to pair outdoor adventure and beer. It's the perfect happy hour—immersing yourself in the natural and urban splendor of Quebec and enjoying a pint with people who are passionate about and proud of their craft.

---

[1] Annual report of the *Association des microbrasseries du Québec*, November 2019.

2

USER GUIDE

PICK YOUR HIKE

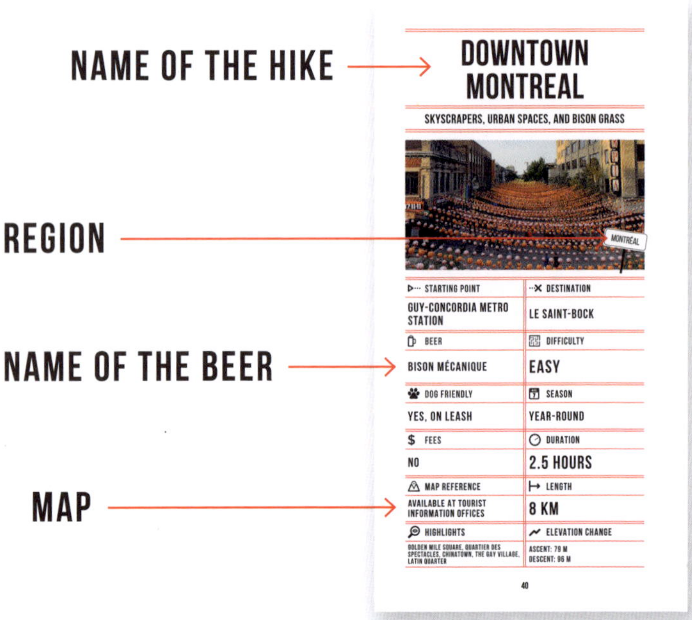

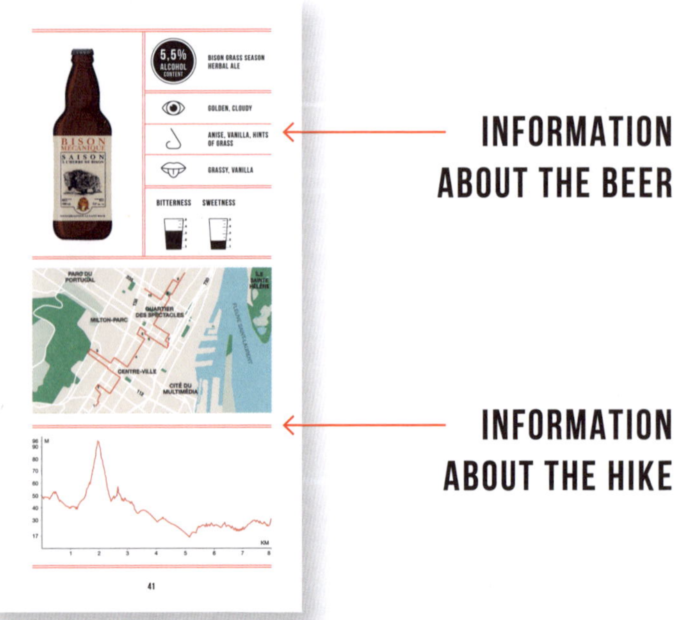

CHOOSING THE TRAILS AND MICROBREWERIES

The trails suggested in this book cover a variety of terrains, lengths, and difficulty levels. Some must-do hikes did not have a nearby brewery and had to be excluded. There were also instances where I had to choose between several interesting options, but the trail I had in mind was closed or unfit for hiking when I was passing through.

Choosing the routes to include in this first edition was no easy task, so I started with what I knew best: microbreweries. First, I drew up a list and eliminated a lot of places right off the bat, such as those without a tap or tasting room, those located in an area ill-suited for hiking, and those lacking noteworthy or accessible trails within a reasonable distance.

Next, I made sure different areas of Quebec were represented. Trails in larger regions and areas more conducive to hiking, such as Gaspé Peninsula (5 hikes) and the Eastern Townships (5 hikes), came up more often. Some areas more popular with tourists—Nunavik, Eeyou Istchee, James Bay, Montérégie, and Laval—were left out. In some cases, there wasn't a regional microbrewery!

Many times, it wasn't until I was on-site that I was able to refine my selection. I often agonized over my decisions. Some features that guided my final picks were terrain variety, the levels of difficulty, the time of the year that trails were open, the number of regions, types of natural beauty, and whether the trails were accessible to most hikers.

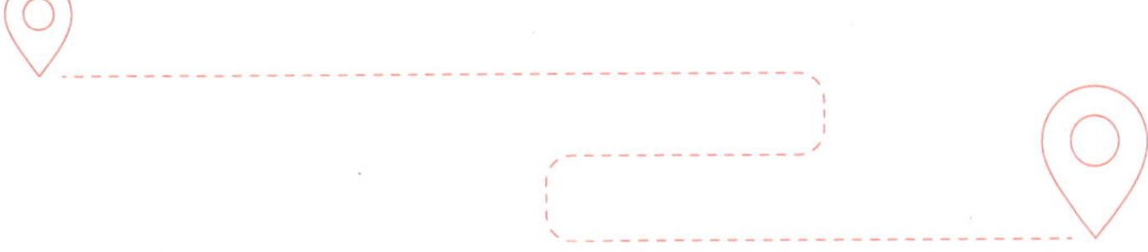

CHOOSING THE BEERS

Choosing the beers was the most difficult part, but I had lots of fun in the process! I was often tempted to just go with a thirst-quenching beer, one that would be perfect after a long hike in the summer heat, but I also had to consider seasonal menu changes and the taste preferences of *la belle province*'s beer enthusiasts. So, picking from a refreshing pale ale, a juicy New England IPA, or a full-bodied stout wasn't always easy.

You can't please everyone. My goal was to pick some crowd-pleasers, with some "funky" brews thrown in, to showcase regional specialties and to explore what makes the beer unique while at the same time choosing a selection that is versatile but neither too disjointed nor homogenous.

For my beer choices and descriptions, I worked with other craft beer enthusiasts familiar with the Quebec market, and I spoke directly to brewmasters.

Moreover, to ensure that the book has a long shelf life, only beers that are on regular offer have been included. That said, menus can change and there is a chance some beers might not be available during your visit. At any rate, I strongly urge you to try limited-edition and seasonal brews as well as collaborations—there's always a hidden gem waiting to be discovered—and finally, to pick your own favorites.

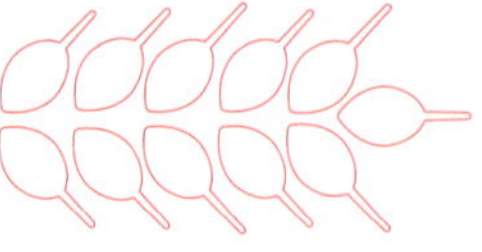

TRAIL DIFFICULTY

The difficulty level given for each hike is an indication only. Ratings are based on trail length, terrain type, and gradient. Bear in mind that the ratings are subjective, are based on the average of all hikes in this book and, in some cases, are made with information provided by trail administrators. It is possible that some sections will present challenges while, for the most part, the trail does not. All details can be found in the trail description.

The perceived level of difficulty also depends on each hiker's physical condition as well as the time of year and the weather conditions. Please note that, for the purpose of preparing this guide, all hikes were completed between June and November.

Easy: A hike listed as easy presents no particular challenge. It is fairly flat, the terrain is suitable for all hikers, and it generally takes less than three hours to complete. These hikes are good for families and require no special preparation.

Moderate: A moderate hike has a well-marked trail and there are no particular dangers. Unlike easy trails, moderate trails may be longer or more uneven, and they may have steep sections. These trails are suitable for the vast majority of people, including children, looking for a bit of exercise.

Strenuous: A strenuous hike is considered difficult if, for example, there are many slopes or it involves a considerable ascent. These hikes are suitable for well-prepared hikers who, ideally, already have some hiking experience and aren't afraid of breaking a sweat.

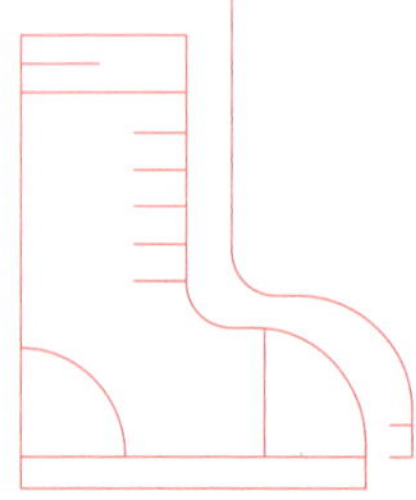

HIKE SMART

Although you don't have to be a seasoned hiker to do the hikes in this book, it's always a good idea to be prepared before hitting the trails, especially when the hike is in a mountainous or forested area.

BEFORE HEADING OUT:

- Find out about trail conditions.
- Pay your access fee, where applicable.
- Let someone in your circle know where you are going.
- Invite someone along. Preferably, don't go alone, especially if there are mountains or woods.
- Check the weather forecast and tide schedule, if applicable.
- Check with the brewery before you take your dog.
- Get the right gear. Ask yourself if you might need the following:
    - A good pair of hiking shoes or boots
    - Clothing that is appropriate for the temperature and weather conditions (Are you climbing a mountain or is the weather likely to be variable?)
    - Extra food and water
    - Mosquito repellent
    - Sunscreen
    - Trail maps
    - A mobile phone (with an external battery or solar charger, as needed)
    - A bag for your trash
    - A first aid kit
        - A head lamp
        - Something to light a fire
        - Survival blankets

WHILE HIKING:

- Know your body and its limits.
- Stay hydratod.
- Respect trail etiquette:
    - Stay off trails that are closed.
    - Respect other hikers.
    - Stick to the trails.
    - Do not approach or feed wildlife.
    - Leave everything as you found it. Don't carry out rocks or branches and don't pick flowers or leaves, etc.
    - Do not litter.
    - Sit on firm surfaces for your breaks (a rock, a tree trunk, etc.) so as not to damage the environment.

SPECIAL PRECAUTIONS

Given the reality of Quebec's seasons and its plant and animal species, you may need to take certain precautions:

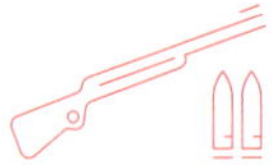

Hunting season. Some trails are closed during hunting season. Some trails require hikers to wear a blaze orange vest. Inquire before you set out.

Wild animals. On some trails, a not-so-delightful encounter with a bear, a moose, a deer, or a lynx might be in store for you. Before you go, learn what to do if you have one.

Poison ivy and giant hogweed. Poison ivy and giant hogweed can be found in some regions. Learn to recognize them and avoid any contact with these plant species.

Mosquitoes. Get a good mosquito repellent. In certain regions and at certain times of the year, mosquitoes can be quite plentiful and surprisingly hungry.

Ticks. Some regions have seen an increase in the number of ticks, which are responsible for transmitting Lyme disease. Inquire before you leave, wear long clothing, use a mosquito repellent, and inspect your skin at the end of the day.

The joys of a Quebec winter. Most of the hikes included in this book can also be done in the winter, with snowshoes or crampons. During winter, however, the trails may differ slightly from how they are described in this book, and their level of difficulty may be higher.

THINK BEFORE YOU DRINK!

When it comes to alcohol, moderation is key. Quebec has an abundance of good beers, but that's no reason to get carried away. For each hike, one beer is recommended. Don't let things get out of hand. As the saying goes, "Boire moins, boire mieux." (Drinking less is better.)

Of course, how much you drink is your decision. So, if you're inclined not to follow this advice, please at least do the following:

- Put down the car keys if you're in no condition to drive.
- Choose a designated driver (and treat them to a non-alcoholic beverage).
- Find out what your local transportation options are (e.g., taxi or pick-up service).
- Take public transit.
- Choose accommodations that are within walking distance of the microbrewery.

USEFUL RESOURCES

Weather conditions and tide schedules:

- The Weather Network (theweathernetwork.com)
- Wind Guru (windguru.cz)
- Tides, currents, and water levels (tides.gc.ca)

Trail conditions: Under each trail description you will find information on where to obtain current trail conditions.

Maps and bearings: The maps included in this book are provided as a guide only. It's recommended that you always get a topographical trail map, especially in areas where there may be no cellular service.

- **Paper maps:** If a paper map is available, you will find where to source it under the trail description. Several maps are available online.
- **Mobile phone maps:** The GPS data files for the hikes presented in this book can be downloaded at Helvetiq.com (or quebec-amerique.com for the French edition). To access these maps, you will need to install a mobile app capable of opening this file type, such as AllTrails, GPsies, or Gaiagps. The choice is yours, as long as it can support GPS Exchange format.

Hiking in Quebec:

- Rando Québec: randoquebec.ca (French only)
- Balise Québec: baliseqc.ca (French only)

Places to hike:

- Société des établissements de plein air du Québec (Sépaq): sepaq.com
- Parks Canada: pc.gc.ca
- L'Association des parcs régionaux du Québec: parq.ca (French only)

Health:

- Lyme disease in Quebec: quebec.ca/en/health/health-issues/a-z/lyme-disease

Safety:

Bear encounters: parks.canada.ca/pn-np/mtn/ours-bears/securite-safety/ours-humains-bears-people

Interesting apps:

- Ondago
- Hikster
- AllTrails

HIKE MAP

30
29
17
9
22
21
20
19
18
8
7
15
6
5
16
23
25
24
26
28
27
2
1
4
3
10
12
14
11
13

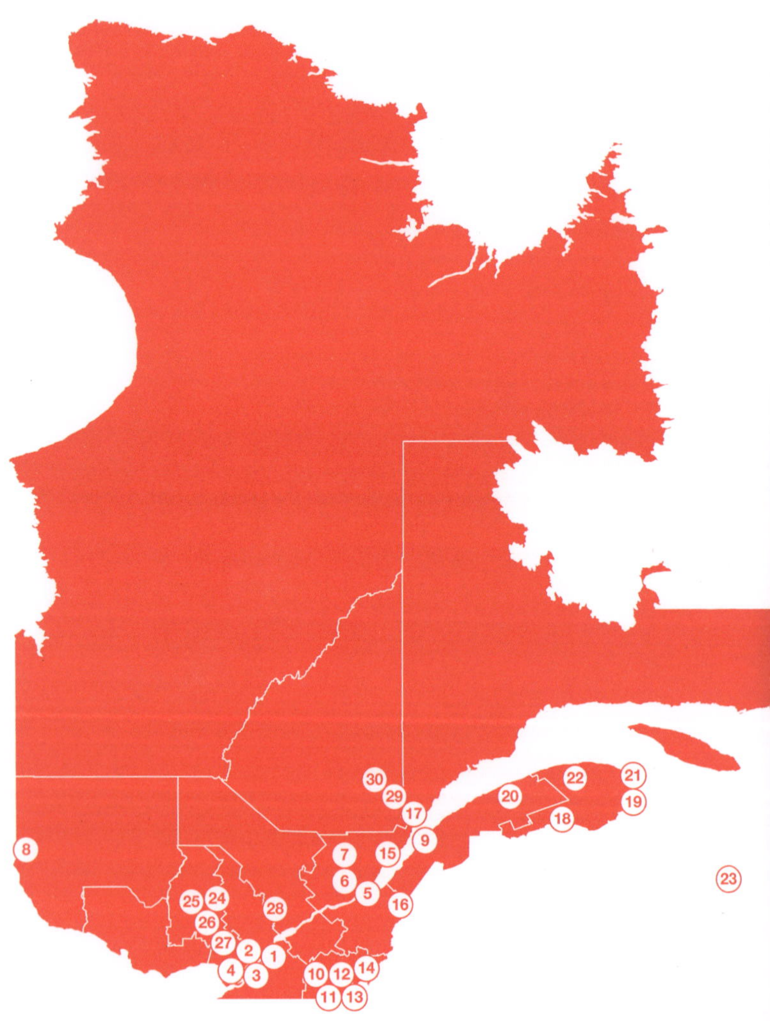

3

BEER HIKES

MONTREAL

OLD MONTREAL AND THE OLD PORT

DISCOVER THE HISTORY OF MONTREAL

STARTING POINT	DESTINATION
CHAMP-DE-MARS METRO STATION	PUB BREWSKEY
BEER	**DIFFICULTY**
P-NUT BUSTER	EASY
DOG FRIENDLY	**SEASON**
YES, ON LEASH	YEAR-ROUND
FEES	**DURATION**
NO	2 HOURS
MAP REFERENCE	**LENGTH**
TOURIST MAP OF OLD MONTREAL AVAILABLE AT TOURIST INFORMATION OR BONSECOURS MARKET	6.7 KM
HIGHLIGHTS	**ELEVATION CHANGE**
NOTRE-DAME BASILICA, OLD PORT, PLACE JACQUES-CARTIER, PLACE D'ARMES	ASCENT: 29 M DESCENT: 33 M

PEANUT BUTTER OAT MILK STOUT

BLACK, HAZY

ROASTED PEANUTS, COFFEE

PEANUTS, VANILLA

BITTERNESS SWEETNESS

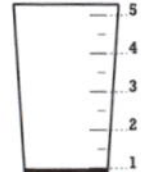

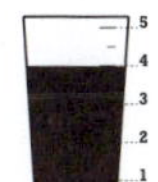

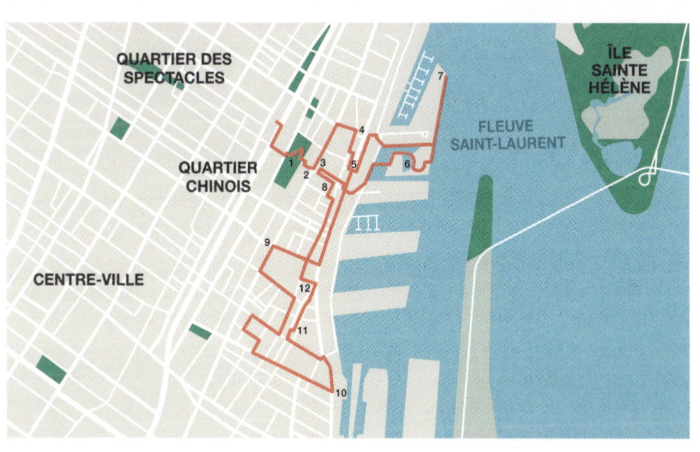

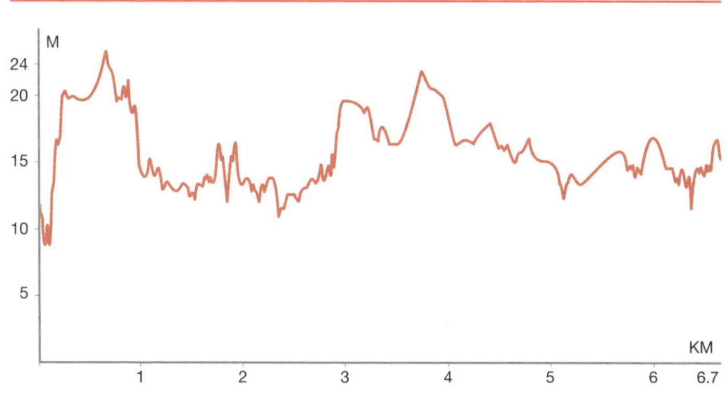

HIKE DESCRIPTION

The neighborhood of Old Montreal, with its narrow, 17th-century cobblestone streets and distinctive architecture, is unlike anything else in the city. As a tourist hotspot that attracts travelers from the four corners of the world, this part of the city is the perfect spot for a delightful stroll. Discover the buzz of an ever-changing neighborhood and a built heritage steeped in history.

The hike starts at the Champ-de-Mars metro station. Head for the exit marked Vieux-Montreal/Saint-Antoine. Once outside, take an immediate right onto the little flagstone lane that darts off at an angle. Walk along it until you reach the sidewalk, then turn left and keep walking until you reach rue Saint-Antoine. Cross rue Saint-Antoine and climb the steps to Champ-de-Mars[1], where you will see the remains of old fortifications.

Go to the other side of the green space and take the stairs leading to Place Vauquelin[2], a square sandwiched between Montreal City Hall and Édifice Lucien-Saulnier, a former courthouse. Go by the fountain and the statue honoring Jean Vauquelin and keep going until you reach the street. Ahead, you will see Place Jacques-Cartier.

You might feel a strong urge to rush off and explore but be patient. Turn left on rue Notre-Dame. On your right, you'll pass Château Ramezay[3], built in 1704–05 and declared a national historic site by the Government of Canada in 1949.

Keep going down rue Notre-Dame until you arrive at rue Bonsecours. Turn right and go down the hill. Ahead, you will see the nearly 300-year-old Notre-Dame-de-Bonsecours Chapel[4]. Turn right on rue Saint-Paul and you will see BreWskey, the delicious destination for this urban hike. But hold your horses—you haven't earned your beer yet!

Just beyond BreWskey is Marché Bonsecours[5], a former public market that now houses several small shops, galleries, and restaurants. Enter the market, turn right, and go to the end of the building. When you get there, exit and take the stairs leading down to the street of the same name.

Turn left toward rue de la Commune. At rue de la Commune, turn left again and walk until you see a sign for the Quai de l'Horloge parking lot. Turn right, cross the railroad tracks, and take the little diagonal path toward the Ferris wheel, the Grande Roue de Montreal[6]. Next, walk along the water and, eventually, the boathouses.

---

[1] This number and those that follow are references to geographic locations on the corresponding hike maps.

When you get to the end, turn left and walk toward the Tour de l'Horloge, or Montreal Clock Tower[7], a memorial to the Canadian sailors who died in World War I. Take some time to look around then walk back to the Ferris wheel. Go around the Grande Roue and then head for the Promenade du Vieux-Port, a boardwalk lined with stands during the summer months.

Turn left onto Promenade du Vieux-Port, strolling back toward rue de la Commune on the right. Cross the street and you'll be at the bottom of Place Jacques-Cartier[8]. This time, go ahead and explore!

Off from Place Jacques-Cartier is rue Saint-Amable, a very quaint street. At the end of rue Saint-Amable is rue Saint-Vincent. Turn left and then turn right onto rue Saint-Paul. Keep going until you get to rue Saint-Sulpice. Turn right. When you reach rue Notre-Dame, cross it and head for Place d'Armes.

Facing the impressive Notre-Dame Basilica[9], head right on rue Notre-Dame. Take a left onto Saint-François-Xavier, then right onto rue Saint-Paul. When you reach rue Saint-Pierre, turn right and walk until you get to rue des Récollets. Turn left and then left again on Sainte-Hélène to head back down.

Go right onto rue Le Moyne. At rue McGill, go left and walk to the end of the street. Among other things, you'll pass by the craft brewery Bistro-Brasserie Les Sœurs Grises, located in an old convent where a good craft beer is always on tap. If you have time, pop in but keep in mind the hike isn't over yet!

At rue de la Commune, turn left. On the other side of the street is another market, Marché des Éclusiers[10].

Keep going down rue de la Commune until you get to rue Marguerite-D'Youville. Take a left at the intersection and then immediately a right onto rue Saint-Pierre. Walk until you reach Place d'Youville[11]. Turn right and walk toward Place Royale.

At Place Royale[12], turn left before turning right onto rue Saint-Paul, then right onto rue Saint-Sulpice. Finally, turn left onto rue de la Commune and head for the BreWskey Pub and Taproom, with entrances on both rue de la Commune and rue Saint-Paul. With this history lesson under your belt, it's time to get down to business and broaden your horizons with a P-Nut Buster, a peanut milk stout (yes, you read that right!).

Notes:
If Bonsecours Market is closed, just continue on to Notre-Dame. If you are doing this hike between May and September, make sure you take time to explore the other market, Marché des Éclusiers.

TRANSPORTATION

The best way to get to Old Montreal is public transit. Both the Place d'Armes and Champ-de-Mars metro stations service this neighborhood. Several bus lines will get you there too. Details can be found on the website of the Société de transport de Montreal (stm.info), the city's public transport agency.

TOURIST INFORMATION

Bureau d'information touristique du Vieux-Montreal (tourist information center)
174 rue Notre-Dame Est (Champ-de-Mars metro station)
Montreal, QC
H2Y 1C2
1 877 BONJOUR
mtl.org

BREWSKEY PUB & TAPROOM

Guillaume Couraud is a whisky and scotch connoisseur who worked in various facets of the restaurant industry across Europe. But it was in an Irish pub that he met his future business partners, Karine Amyotte and Derrick Robertson. BreWskey Pub opened in 2015 as a gathering place where patrons could immediately feel at home, even though it's located in a heavy tourist area. Four years later, the taproom was added so they could brew their beers on-site and welcome an increasingly loyal customer base. In addition to celebrating beer, BreWskey only serves Canadian alcohol, most of which comes from Quebec.

BREWERY

BreWskey Pub & Taproom
380 rue Saint-Paul Est
Montreal, QC
H2Y 1H3
514 507-2739
brewskey.ca

NEARBY BREWERY

Bistro-brasserie Les Sœurs Grises
32 rue McGill
Montreal, QC
H2Y 3W5
514 788-7635
bblsg.com

WHERE TO TRY THIS BEER

Right on-site.

WHERE TO BUY THIS BEER

You can buy all your favorite beers on-site.

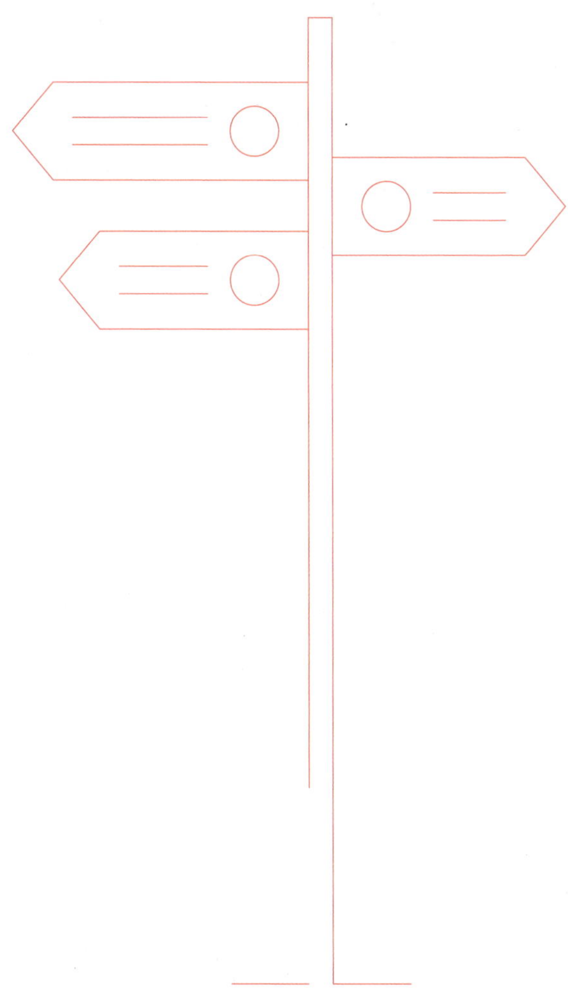

PLATEAU-MONT-ROYAL

FROM THE ECLECTIC PLATEAU TO THE ELECTRIC MILE END

STARTING POINT	DESTINATION
MONT-ROYAL METRO STATION	HELM MICROBRASSERIE
BEER	**DIFFICULTY**
HUTCHIE BLONDIE	MODERATE
DOG FRIENDLY	**SEASON**
YES, ON LEASH	YEAR-ROUND
FEES	**DURATION**
NO	3.5 HOURS
MAP REFERENCE	**LENGTH**
AVAILABLE AT VARIOUS LOCAL SHOPS	11.7 KM
HIGHLIGHTS	**ELEVATION CHANGE**
PLATEAU-MONT-ROYAL, STREET ART (MURALS), LA FONTAINE PARK, SAINT-LOUIS SQUARE, MILE END, GREEN ALLEYWAYS	ASCENT: 58 M DESCENT: 37 M

WEST COAST IPA

ORANGEY, CLEAR

CITRUS

CITRUS, HOPS

BITTERNESS

SWEETNESS

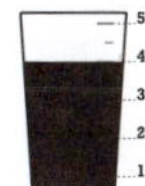

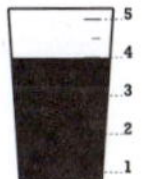

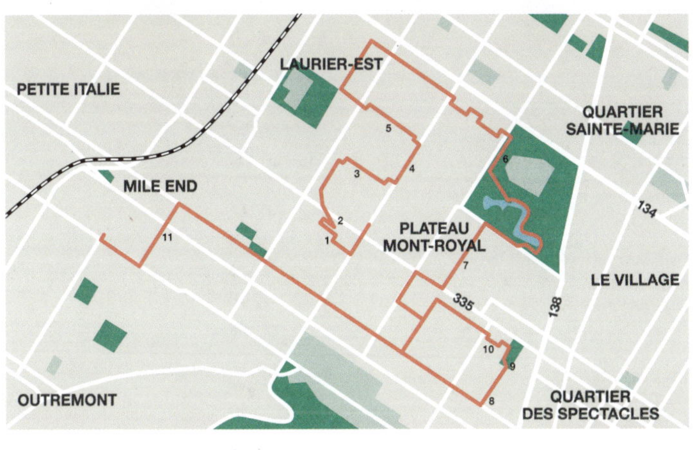

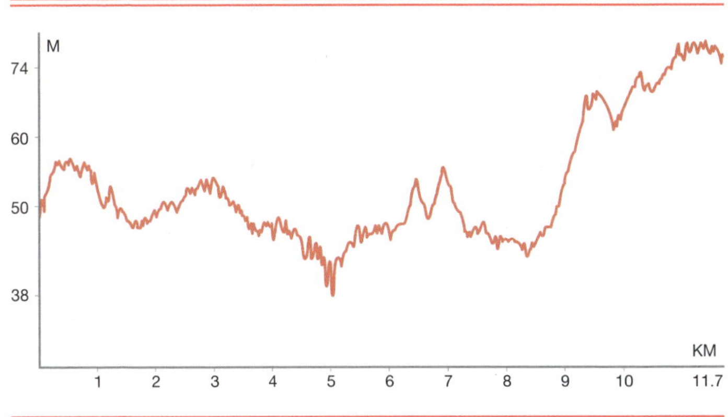

HIKE DESCRIPTION

Here you are, in the heart of Montreal, at the famous Plateau-Mont-Royal. It's easy to fall in love with this neighborhood and its pretty, colorful houses and green alleyways that provide a soothing escape from the hustle and bustle of the city. There are incredible works of street art and the area has a unique vibe—young, hip, happening—that adds to its appeal.

This 12-kilometer urban hike is a chance to discover the plateau via busy thoroughfares, green spaces, and friendly pedestrian streets. Your adventure starts at the Mont-Royal metro station and ends in the Mile End neighborhood. The tour is peppered with striking works of street art, so don't forget to look up from time to time to admire them.

As you exit the Mont-Royal metro station, turn left onto avenue Mont-Royal and walk until you get to avenue Henri-Julien. Turn right and keep going until you arrive at rue Gilford. Make a right onto rue Gilford[1] and head toward rue Drolet where you'll hang a left. Turn right onto rue Villeneuve and then right again onto rue de Grand-Pré. This will lead you back to Gilford, where you will take a left.

When you reach rue Saint-Denis, cross the street, walk a few meters, turn left and continue onto the next section of Gilford[2], a pedestrian area that breaks with Montreal's usual quadrangular-street layout and instead follows the old Chemin des Carrières. Veer slightly to the right, cross the divider, and continue to follow rue Gilford, stretching out before you.

When you get to Saint-André, turn right and duck into the first little lane you see on your left. Take a quick right and follow the green alleyway[3] wedged between rue Saint-André and rue de Mentana.

Turn left onto rue de Bienville, then right at rue de Mentana. Walk until you reach avenue Mont-Royal[4].

Turn left at Mont-Royal and keep going until rue de Brébeuf. Hang a left and take the first street on your right and then turn left. Now, you are in another of the green alleyways[5] typical of the neighborhood. When you reach rue Gilford, turn left and then go right onto rue de Brébeuf.

Cross boulevard Saint-Joseph and go straight toward avenue Laurier. Need to fill up your water bottle or go to the bathroom? Sir Wilfrid Laurier Park is on the other side of avenue Laurier, so take advantage!

Turn right onto Laurier until you get to rue Fabre. Turn right and walk until you reach La Fontaine Park. During that walk, you can stay on rue Fabre or zigzag among the various streets and alleyways: for instance, rue Marquette/Fabre, which is especially pretty. Your goal is simply to get to La Fontaine Park, about 450 meters away.

You should now be on rue Rachel with La Fontaine Park[6], one of the oldest green spaces in Montreal, in front of you. Enter the park, veer right, and pass the two children's play areas to get to a short avenue called Calixa-Lavallée. From there, cross the park and take one of the trails to get to the lower pond. You will pass by a monument honoring Félix Leclerc, one of Quebec's most celebrated singer-songwriters (as well as actor and poet), and the old gatehouse of the Jardin des Merveilles (Garden of Wonders). When you're next to the water, head left and follow the path to the other side. At the end, go up the stairs, turn right, and follow avenue Parc-La Fontaine. When you get to rue Duluth[7], cross the street and take it.

Keep going on Duluth as far as Saint-Denis where you will turn right and then left onto Rachel. Walk along rue Rachel. Take a moment to admire Église Saint-Jean-Baptiste (St. John the Baptist Church) on the right. Pass avenue Laval and turn at the first little alleyway on your left. There, you'll discover another little green oasis—and a much-needed boost.

At Duluth, go right and walk until you meet up with boulevard Saint-Laurent. You will pass Le Réservoir, a local brewery you might want to check out. You do deserve a break, but the hike isn't over yet, so save some energy for the rest of the walk!

Turn left on boulevard Saint-Laurent. From here, keep your eyes peeled for all the beautiful murals that make Montreal such a creative, flamboyant city. Keep going on this busy boulevard for about 850 meters and then hang a left onto rue Prince-Arthur-Est[8], a pedestrian street. You'll walk by the Dispensaire de Bière, where some of the finest craft beers are brewed.

Keep going until you reach Square Saint-Louis[9]. Go in and look around. In the middle of the square, you'll see some welcome greenery surrounded by brightly colored Victorian houses. Next to the most colorful ones, you'll find rue Drolet. Take it. The first little exit on your left leads to a lane (immediately on your right) with a country feel[10]: a tiny, urban gem where nature and community reign supreme.

These green alleyways came about when citizens joined forces to demand, among other things, better air quality, rainwater capture, a reduction in noise pollution and heat islands, and increased biodiversity. Such locations, referred to as *champêtre* (meaning "country" or "rustic"), lack asphalt and are closed to vehicular traffic.

At the end of the alleyway, turn right, back onto rue Drolet and then turn left. Keep going until you hit Duluth. Go left. Seem familiar? It should, because you were here earlier!

Once you hit the intersection at boulevard Saint-Laurent, look up and there is Mount Royal Cross rising proudly before you (for more info, see the Mount Royal Park hike). Turn right and you're in for another treat of murals, each one more impressive than the last.

As you stroll down boulevard Saint-Laurent, you'll cross three consecutive parks to take a breather and admire the beauty of your surroundings: Parc des Amériques, Parc du Portugal, and Parc Lahaie. At the intersection with avenue Laurier Est, you'll find the microbrewery Siboire. But it's not your destination, so keep going. You're almost there!

Keep going on boulevard Saint-Laurent until you arrive at Saint-Viateur[11]. Turn left and when you reach avenue du Parc, take a right. At rue Bernard, take another right. Now, you've arrived at your destination: HELM is located on your left, and a warm welcome awaits.

Notes:
In winter, some streets may be icy or snow covered, especially the alleyways and certain trails in La Fontaine Park. Check conditions before heading out or skip these locations if necessary.

Other options:
If street art is your thing, get a free mural map at muralfestival.com. The streets and alleyways around boulevard Saint-Laurent are especially notable for their incredible artwork, so be sure to revisit them when you have a chance.

TRANSPORTATION

The Mont-Royal metro station is the easiest and quickest way to get to this neighborhood. You'll also find plenty of self-service BIXI bike rentals and well-serviced bus lines in this area. At the end of your hike, you can hop back on the metro at Outremont station.

TOURIST INFORMATION

Centre Infotouriste de Montreal
1442 rue Clark
1 877 BONJOUR
bonjourquebec.com

HELM MICROBRASSERIE

HELM (an acronym for the French words *hops, water, yeast*, and *malt)* has been in operation since 2006 but its image and approach have evolved. Now it is a Mile End institution—they care for the beer they produce, and it shows. You can taste the English inspiration in each beer Sébastien Brisson, head brewer, makes. While he isn't afraid to think outside the box, he never strays from his respect for the ingredients or his neighborhood. In fact, Sébastien's neighborhood pride is reflected in the names of his beers.

BREWERY

HELM Microbrasserie
273 rue Bernard Ouest
Montreal, QC H2V 1T5
514 276-0473
helmmicrobrasserie.ca

NEARBY BREWERIES

Le Réservoir
9 avenue Duluth Est
Montreal, QC H2W 1G7
514 849-7779
reservoirbrasseur.com

Le Dispensaire de Bières
32 rue Prince Arthur Est
Montreal, QC H2X 1B5
514 307-0855
dispensairedebiere.com

Siboire
5101 boulevard Saint-Laurent
Montreal, QC H2T 1R9
514 379-3633
siboire.ca/saint-laurent

WHERE TO TRY THIS BEER

Most HELM beers can be tasted only on-site, although some are distributed in cans or bottles.

WHERE TO BUY THIS BEER

Veux-tu une bière? (Specialty shop)
5105 boulevard Saint-Laurent
Montreal, QC
H2T 1R9
514 871-2663

DOWNTOWN MONTREAL

SKYSCRAPERS, URBAN SPACES, AND BISON GRASS

STARTING POINT	DESTINATION
GUY-CONCORDIA METRO STATION	LE SAINT-BOCK
BEER	**DIFFICULTY**
BISON MÉCANIQUE	EASY
DOG FRIENDLY	**SEASON**
YES, ON LEASH	YEAR-ROUND
FEES	**DURATION**
NO	2.5 HOURS
MAP REFERENCE	**LENGTH**
AVAILABLE AT TOURIST INFORMATION OFFICES	8 KM
HIGHLIGHTS	**ELEVATION CHANGE**
GOLDEN MILE SQUARE, QUARTIER DES SPECTACLES, CHINATOWN, THE GAY VILLAGE, LATIN QUARTER	ASCENT: 79 M DESCENT: 96 M

BISON GRASS SEASON HERBAL ALE

GOLDEN, CLOUDY

ANISE, VANILLA, HINTS OF GRASS

GRASSY, VANILLA

BITTERNESS

SWEETNESS

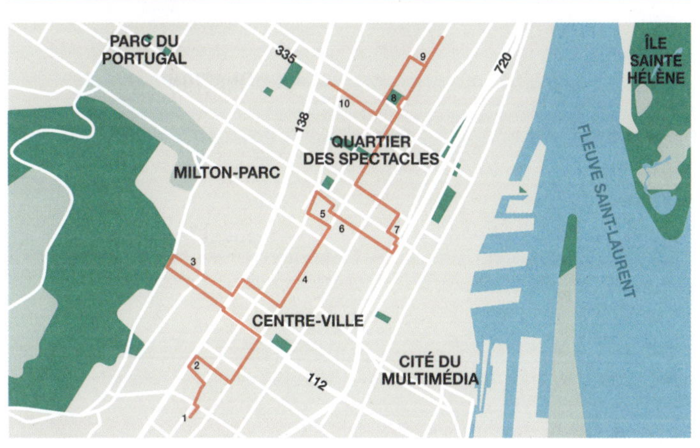

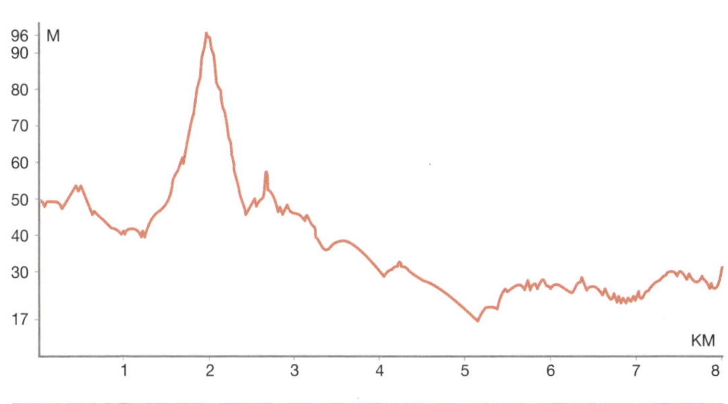

HIKE DESCRIPTION

Multicultural, lively, upscale, and working-class: The varied neighborhoods that make up downtown Montreal are utterly urban in their own unique way. Step into a new world with each new kilometer.

The hike starts at the intersection of rue Guy and boulevard de Maisonneuve where the Guy-Concordia metro station is located. You are immediately plunged deep into the Golden Square Mile, an affluent neighborhood known for its merchant-class, Victorian-era homes that bear witness to the wealthy past of Montreal's elite. The area also boasts many museums. It is said that, at the turn of the 20th century, 80% of Canada's wealth was concentrated in Golden Square Mile.

Turn right on boulevard de Maisonneuve toward Place Norman-Bethune[1]. Keep going until you get to rue Bishop. Turn left and continue until you reach Sherbrooke. Straight ahead is the Church of St. Andrew and St. Paul, a Presbyterian church.

Turn right onto Sherbrooke. The Montreal Museum of Fine Arts[2] is on your right. Pass the museum and turn right onto lively rue Crescent. Continue as far as rue Sainte-Catherine and take the opportunity to wave to Leonard Cohen (if you don't see him, look higher).

At Sainte-Catherine, turn left and then left again when you get to Peel. Here you will go up to avenue des Pins (where the hike in Mount Royal Park begins).

Turn right onto avenue des Pins. When you get to rue McTavish, turn right. After crossing avenue du Docteur-Penfield, take the steps down to a pedestrian street and keep going straight. You are now on the campus of the famous McGill University, where the architecture alone is worth the trip. Don't hesitate to take the short paths between the buildings, including the one leading to the Redpath Museum[3].

Take your time. Turn left onto rue Sherbrooke and then right onto avenue McGill-College. Stay on McGill-College until you connect again with rue Sainte-Catherine. Turn left and get lost among the skyscrapers of Montreal. One by one, you'll pass the Anglican Christ Church Cathedral, Phillips Square[4], and St. James United Church.

At rue Jeanne-Mance, turn left. You're now in the Quartier des Spectacles[5], the arts and entertainment district, where you'll see the Montreal Symphony House and the Place des Arts promenade. Before getting back on Sainte-Catherine, take some time to explore and soak up the area's artsy vibe as you meander among the buildings.

Return to rue Sainte-Catherine. Across the street is the Complexe Desjardins[6]. Have you ever heard of Montreal's underground? Does it

sound shady? Well, it's time to pull back the curtains and explore just one part of the 33 km network of underground passages.[2]

Enter the Complexe Desjardins from the Sainte-Catherine side and head downstairs to the food court. Now it's time to find the Convention Center (Palais des Congrès). Go down, go straight, and keep going toward Complexe Guy-Favreau. Find the Service Canada offices and then follow the signs to the Convention Center. Once at the Convention Center, take the escalator down. To your left, you'll see the Place d'Armes metro station and, straight ahead, a small shopping gallery where there's an exit onto rue Saint-Urbain.

So, now you're on Saint-Urbain. Head left and a few dozen meters farther you'll notice a big change in scenery: Chinatown[7]! This is one of the oldest Asian districts in North America. Go past avenue Viger and then take rue de la Gauchetière to your right.

Now take boulevard Saint-Laurent on your left and go back up as far as Sainte-Catherine (yes, her again!). Go right and you'll cross part of the campus of the Université du Québec à Montreal (UQAM). On your left, find Émilie-Gamelin Park[8] (just past the Berri-UQAM metro station). Look around the park and then get back on Sainte-Catherine. Keep going on Sainte-Catherine toward the Gay Village[9] and its rainbow colors.

Stay on Sainte-Catherine for a bit and then turn left onto rue Atateken, a Mohawk name that pays homage to the city's Indigenous heritage. Next, take a left onto boulevard de Maisonneuve.

At the intersection with rue Saint-Denis, turn right, and you're in for yet another change of atmosphere: the Latin Quarter[10].

Le Saint-Bock microbrewery is on your right, and it's time to sit back and enjoy the excitement of your surroundings, as you sip a delicious Bison Mécanique (Mechanical Bison). If you're in the mood, there are other breweries in the neighborhood to check out, such as L'Amère à Boire (French speakers love the play on words), located about 130 meters away.

Notes:
When you get to the Gay Village, why not keep going on Sainte-Catherine if it looks worth checking out. To get back on track, just retrace your steps and take rue Atateken on your right.

TRANSPORTATION

As indicated, the easiest way to get around Montreal is to use public transit. Get off at Guy-Concordia metro station. At the end of your journey, the Sherbrooke and Berri-UQAM stations are reasonably close. You can also hop onto a bus. Check the Société de transport de Montreal website (stm.info) for routes and schedules.

TOURIST INFORMATION

Centre Infotouriste
1255 Peel Street
Suite 100 (Peel Metro Station)
Montreal, QC
H3B 4V4
1 877 BONJOUR
mtl.org

[2] In reality, the underground is more of a curiosity than a must-do, and because access can be restricted for one reason or another, you can bypass the underground by following these directions: from Place des Festivals, facing Complexe Desjardins, turn right onto Sainte-Catherine. When you get to Jeanne-Mance, turn left and go as far as avenue Viger. There, go left until you get to rue Saint-Urbain.

LE SAINT-BOCK

Le Saint-Bock (or holy beer glass) was established by Martin Guimond in 2006 and, for a time, it was one of the largest beer bars in the world. A few hundred different craft beers are on offer, many of which are brewed on-site. It's this inspirational setting that allows the imaginations of brewmasters Julien Savoie and Philippe Tremblay to run wild. Whether it's the Malédiction beer served up with a marshmallow or the way some of the beers find their way into the food, Guimond's creativity and passion—as well as the entire team's commitment to serving a good brew—is plain to see.

BREWERY

Le Saint-Bock
1749 rue Saint-Denis
Montreal, QC
H2X 3K4
514 680-8052
saintbock.com

NEARBY BREWERY

L'Amère à Boire
2049 rue Saint-Denis
Montreal, QC
H2X 3K8
514 282-7448
amereaboire.com

WHERE TO TRY THIS BEER

On-site, on a "terrasse" (even English-speaking Montrealers call patios terrasses!), or inside. Le Saint-Bock also serves pub grub.

WHERE TO BUY THIS BEER

At several retail outlets in the area and throughout the province.

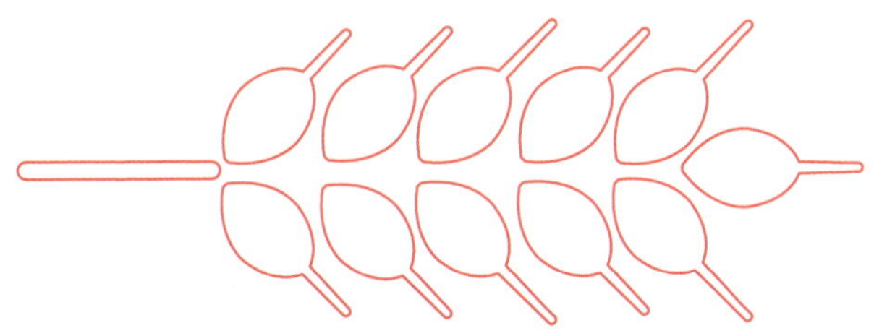

MOUNT ROYAL PARK

A BREATH OF FRESH AIR IN THE HEART OF THE CITY

STARTING POINT	DESTINATION
PEEL METRO STATION	DIEU DU CIEL!
BEER	**DIFFICULTY**
HIBISCUS DEW	MODERATE
DOG FRIENDLY	**SEASON**
YES, ON LEASH	YEAR-ROUND
FEES	**DURATION**
NO	2.5 HOURS
MAP REFERENCE	**LENGTH**
AVAILABLE AT TOURIST INFORMATION OFFICES	7.5 KM
HIGHLIGHTS	**ELEVATION CHANGE**
MOUNT ROYAL CROSS, KONDIARONK LOOKOUT, VIEW OF DOWNTOWN, CAMILLIEN-HOUDE LOOKOUT	ASCENT: 252 M DESCENT: 231 M

HIBISCUS FLOWER WHEAT BEER

ROSÉ

FLORAL HINTS, RED BERRIES

FRUITY, FLORAL, TART

BITTERNESS

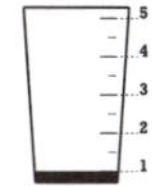

SWEETNESS

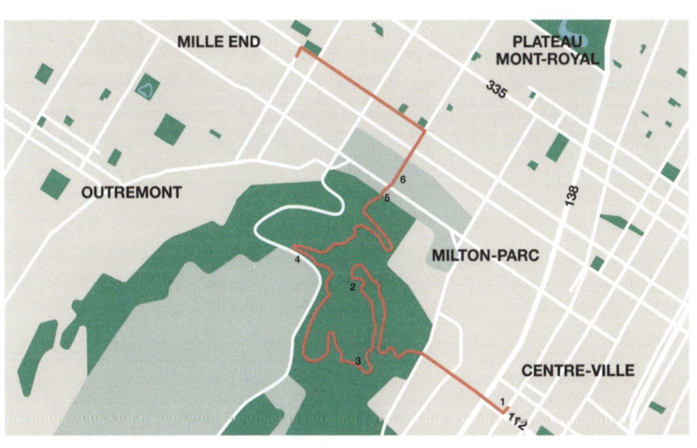

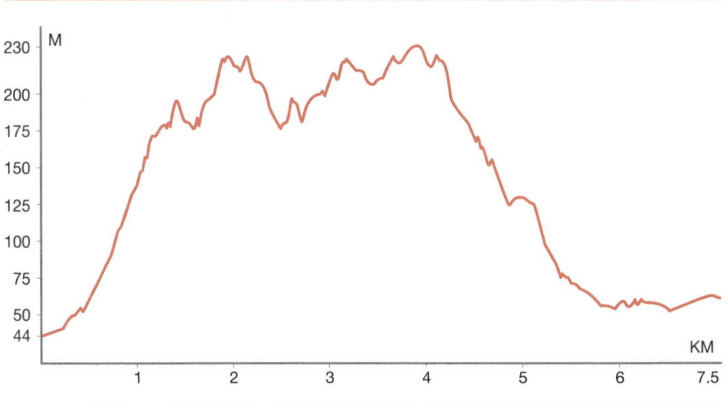

HIKE DESCRIPTION

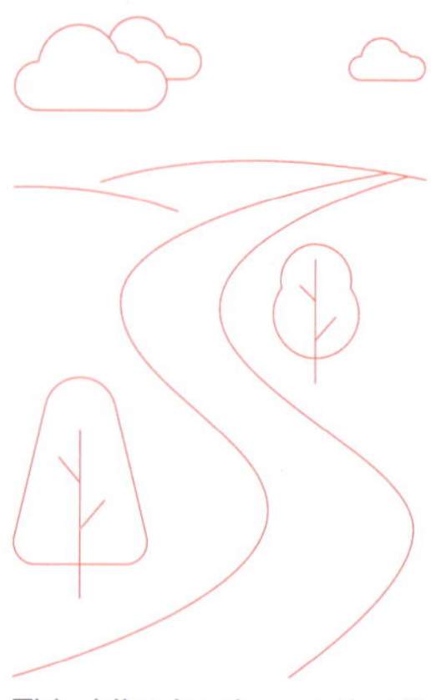

Looking out over Montreal's downtown, Mount Royal Park was designed by Frederick Law Olmsted, the landscape architect who designed New York City's Central Park. Mount Royal Park is a meeting place for Montrealers looking for a slice of nature and a must-see for tourists. Well serviced by public transit, the park is spread over 190 hectares, with more than twenty kilometers of walking trails. Mount Royal Park also has three different summits, including the main 233-meter-high peak for which it is named.

This hike begins at the Peel metro station[1]. Take the Peel exit and go north on rue Peel, crossing a section of the McGill University campus, until you get to avenue des Pins. Cross the street and take the stairs in front of you.

In the middle of the steep set of stairs (with 399 steps that will take you directly to Mount Royal lookout), you'll see a trail, Sentier de l'Escarpement[2], on the right, about 100 meters past Chemin Olmsted. Go ahead and take it, getting away from the crowds while enjoying the views of the city. You'll get to the top a little later. Promise!

Follow the signs to Mount Royal Cross[3] (and get a different view than that from the Plateau-Mont-Royal hike). The signs are not always obvious—know that the cross is to your left and if you see a set of stairs, you've gone too far. After visiting the cross, connect with the Boucle du Sommet and follow the loop until you get to the lookout.

The trail will then lead you gently to Mount Royal Chalet and Kondiaronk Lookout[4]. Chances are there'll be a crowd, but make your way through and take in Montreal from high up. The view is especially stunning at day's end when the city slowly begins to light up.

Head left to the other side of the chalet and keep going until the intersection. Take a right to get back on the Boucle du Sommet. This trail goes on for a considerable distance. There'll be some interesting views of another part of the city as you go around the mountain. Next stop: Camillien-Houde lookout[5].

With the Camillien-Houde lookout behind you, head immediately into the woods on your right, and then stay right on the trail until it intersects with Chemin Olmsted. Turn left and go farther down until you see the Sir George Étienne Cartier Monument[6] on your right. Turn toward it.

Cross the square, avenue du Parc, and then Jeanne-Mance Park. Keep going on rue Rachel until you get to boulevard Saint-Laurent. There, turn left and keep straight until you get to avenue Laurier. Take a left. The microbrewery Dieu du Ciel! is on your right. It's time to go in and get that Hibiscus Dew.

Notes:
In winter, while Chemin Olmsted is sure to be open, some sections might be inaccessible. Check before heading out and stay off closed trails.

Some trails have good signage but others, not so much. In any case, it's hard to get lost on Mount Royal. If in doubt, just get back on Chemin

Olmsted and you can't go wrong. For a better experience, take along a trail map.

Other options:
Keep in mind that Mount Royal has many, many trails, not all of which will be shown on your map. As a result, there are many ways to get from point A to point B and it's easy to prolong the experience—check out Beaver Lake, for instance.

TRANSPORTATION

Start this hike at the Peel metro station. The Laurier and Mont-Royal metro stations are just a few minutes' walk from where your hike ends.

TRAIL INFORMATION

Les amis de la montagne (Friends of the Mountain)
514 843-8240
lemontroyal.qc.ca

TOURIST INFORMATION

Centre Infotouriste
1255 Peel Street
Suite 100
Peel Metro Station
514 873-2015
mtl.org

DIEU DU CIEL!

While studying biology, Jean-François Gravel, now a brewmaster, began experimenting with home brew. It was at this time that he met Stéphane Ostiguy, a student pursuing a master's degree in applied microbiology. Eventually, a pastime became a passion and in 1998 they established Dieu du Ciel! (translated as *God in heaven* but more closely akin to *my goodness*). Today, Dieu du Ciel! is a renowned brewery, and the pair's penchant for bold brews comes through in each of their high-quality beers. This brewpub, with its excellent location and extensive food menu, offers a wide variety of home brews that are sure to please any beer lover's palate.

BREWERY

Dieu du Ciel !
29 avenue Laurier
Montreal QC
H2T 2N2
514 490-9555
dieuduciel.com

WHERE TO TRY THIS BEER

Right on-site. Don't forget to eat!

WHERE TO BUY THIS BEER

Veux-tu une bière ? (Specialty store)
5105 boulevard Saint-Laurent
Montreal, QC H2T 1R9
514 871-2633

Dieu du Ciel! beers are sold in several stores throughout the province. The brewpub also sells growlers to take out.

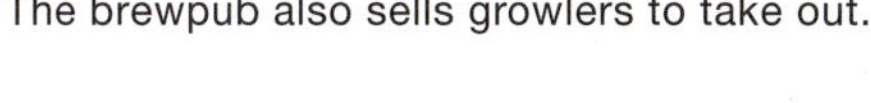

QUEBEC CITY AND SURROUNDING AREA

QUEBEC CITY

HISTORICAL HUB WITH A DOWNTOWN BUZZ

STARTING POINT	DESTINATION
THE BATTLEFIELDS PARK	NOCTEM, ARTISANS BRASSEURS
BEER	**DIFFICULTY**
CATNIP	MODERATE
DOG FRIENDLY	**SEASON**
YES, ON LEASH	YEAR-ROUND
FEES	**DURATION**
NO	3 HOURS
MAP REFERENCE	**LENGTH**
AVAILABLE AT TOURIST INFORMATION OFFICES	10.5 KM
HIGHLIGHTS	**ELEVATION CHANGE**
THE BATTLEFIELDS PARK, CITADELLE OF QUEBEC, CHÂTEAU FRONTENAC, OLD QUEBEC	ASCENT: 167 M DESCENT: 243 M

AMERICAN IPA

YELLOW, CLOUDY

CITRUS, MANGO

FRUITY, CITRUS AND MANGO HINTS, HOPPY

BITTERNESS

SWEETNESS

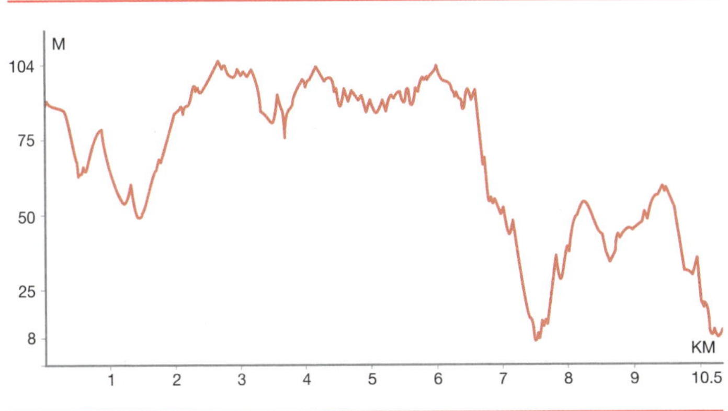

HIKE DESCRIPTION

Quebec City is perfectly walkable. This urban hike is a journey through history and before it's over, you'll be catapulted into the hustle and bustle of a downtown core that is ever-changing.

If you do this hike in winter, make sure to read the notes below as some sections will be modified.

The journey starts at the entrance to The Battlefields Park, where Grande-Allée and avenue Montcalm meet. Right in front of you are the Plains of Abraham[1], a large area of land and a circular asphalt track. Follow the bike path running parallel to avenue Montcalm and turn right where the path intersects with Côte Gilmour Hill. There, you'll see interpretative panels with information about the area's history and the trail itself. Head down to the little wooded trail on your left, which turns into the Sentier de la nature (Nature Trail).

The Nature Trail[2] provides a great opportunity to learn about the area's plant life thanks to information boards that recount the story of the country's first herbalists. At the fork, keep right and continue to follow signage for the Nature Trail. At the next junction, follow the signs toward the Pavilion (services building) on your left.

As you leave the wooded area, onto avenue Ontario, go left and then immediately turn right onto avenue Garneau. Head up to the Pavilion[3]. If you're lucky, you might be treated to a free, open-air concert at the Edwin-Bélanger Bandstand.

Get back on the road behind the Pavilion, which is practically the backyard of Quebec's provincial museum of fine arts, Le Musée national des beaux-arts du Québec. Keep going until you get to a fork in the road and take the promenade that runs parallel to avenue George VI. You'll walk right past the spot where Major-General James Wolfe was delivered his fatal blow. Don't forget to pay attention to the period architecture or look for Martello Tower 1[4], which is your next destination. The view of the St. Lawrence River makes the few steps up well worth the effort. Now, turn back and take the paved path overlooking Cap Diamant (a cape on the promontory of Quebec City) toward the Château Frontenac.

When you arrive at a sign, keep going straight and through the trees, veering slightly to the right until you get to another paved road. Straight ahead is the top of a staircase, the Escalier du Cap-Blanc[5]. Construction on this staircase started in 1868, and with 398 steps, it is the longest in Quebec City.

To the left of the stairs, climb up the little hill (the trampled, dirt paths will point the way) to get to avenue du Cap-Diamant[6]. Follow this street as far as the kiosk[7], which offers another nice view of the river. Along the way, you'll see the ruins of an old bunker. From the kiosk, follow the paved road to the military museum. At the first opportunity, climb up on the ramparts[8] on your right and follow the trail around the Citadelle[9].

When you get to the end, there'll be a breathtaking view of the Dufferin Terrace, the Château Frontenac, and the St. Lawrence River. On a clear day, you can see the Île d'Orléans Bridge in the distance. The view echoes a true painting, so make sure you take it all in before turning back.

Once back at the kiosk, take Promenade des Gouverneurs[10], a wooden boardwalk tucked between a cliff and the river, that leads to the Dufferin Terrace[11], which you will cross. Once past the monument to Samuel de Champlain, and the funicular, head down the Frontenac stairs and take a right onto Côte de la Montagne. On your right, take the Escalier Casse-Cou[12], also known as Breakneck Steps (don't let the name frighten you), for a glimpse of the famous Quartier du Petit Champlain[13] area.

Keep going straight until you arrive at the Petit-Champlain fresco and then, when you reach boulevard Champlain, turn left. Go straight and turn left onto rue Cul-de-Sac (which is not a dead-end street, as the name implies) and follow it to the end before turning left onto rue Notre-Dame. In no time, you'll arrive at a hotspot for history and architecture buffs:Notre-Dame-des-Victoires church and Place Royale[14]. Take some time to poke around, and then keep going straight until you get to Côte de la Montagne, where you'll go left to get back up to Old Quebec.

Go through Prescott Gate (you were there earlier). A few meters beyond, on the right, enter Parc de la Chute-Montmorency[15], a national historic site that was first a cemetery, then a hub of civil and religious power, and finally a strategic military site. Take a stroll around the park and check out the cannons. There are also statues of George-Étienne Cartier (one of the Fathers of Confederation) and Louis Hébert (the first European apothecary in the region).

Exit the same way you came in. Then cross the street and take the stairs leading up to the Passage du Chien-d'Or, an alleyway located between the statue of François de Laval and the post office building.

Cross rue du Fort and continue on rue de Buade before turning left onto rue du Trésor[16]. Enjoy the street's artistic flair before turning right and then right again onto rue des Jardins. Facing away from city hall, cross the square of the same name (Place de l'Hôtel-de-Ville)[17] and admire Notre-Dame-de-Québec Basilica-Cathedral[18], located on the other side. Get on Côte de la Fabrique[19], which eventually veers left and becomes rue Saint-Jean[20]. Keep going as far as the Fortifications of Quebec National Historic Site (on the left) and go through Saint-Jean Gate.

Now you've reached Place d'Youville[21], flanked by a theater, Le Théâtre Capitole, and a concert hall, the Palais Montcalm. This is the Saint-Jean-Baptiste neighborhood, one of Quebec City's oldest. Keep going straight and cross avenue Honoré-Mercier. You will pass the Claire-Martin library, located in the former St. Matthew's Anglican Church[22], and a cemetery of the same name. Head for Côte Sainte-Geneviève[23] and turn right.

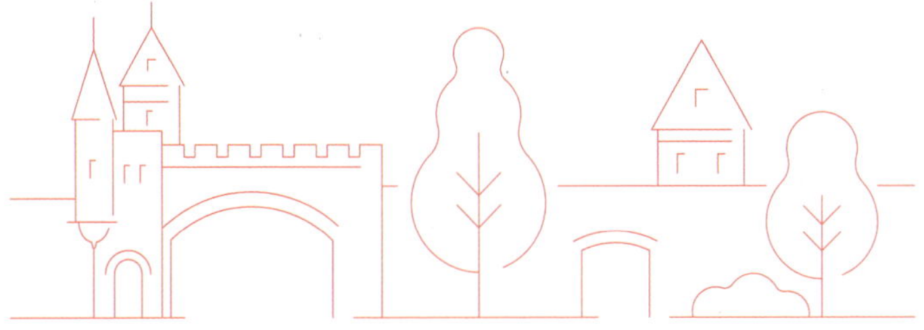

At the end of the street, veer left, stay on rue Saint-Réal[24] and go straight ahead until you arrive, on your right, at the Ascenseur du Faubourg, an elevator you'll be tempted to hop on, but don't! Instead, take the stairs[25] (you're going to earn that beer!) and then cut at an angle through Jardin Jean-Paul-L'Allier[26], a city square and garden, to get to rue du Parvis. There, hang a left and cross boulevard Charest. You've arrived at your destination: Noctem Artisans Brasseurs[27]. Time to taste one of their flagship beers: the Catnip.

Notes:
If you want to check out another brewery, try La Korrigane not far from there.

Winter option:
In winter, follow the Nature Trail to the very end, in the direction of the Citadelle. You'll pass below the Martello Tower, near the staircase, Escalier du Cap-Blanc. Then turn right and follow the signs to the Terrasse des Gouverneurs. Skip the Citadelle part of the hike and instead jump right onto Promenade des Gouverneurs boardwalk.

TRANSPORTATION

Check the RTC (Réseau de transport de la capitale) bus schedule for the beginning and end of the hike. If you're traveling by car, park on one of the small streets adjacent to The Battlefields Park or at the parking lot, near the entrance, and take the bus back.

TOURIST INFORMATION

Office de tourisme de Québec
12 rue Sainte-Anne
Quebec City, QC G1R 3X2
1 877 BONJOUR
quebec-cite.com

NOCTEM ARTISANS BRASSEURS

Time to swap brew water for maple sap, or try a stout made with hot peppers and grapefruit. The collective imagination of Brian Pierce, Yann Gravel, and Jean-Michaël Noël knows no bounds. The trio began dabbling in the art of brewing when they were university students, and what started out as a hobby among pals turned into one serious business idea. In 2015, Noctem Artisans Brasseurs was born, and it has been known for the quality and originality of its IPAs ever since (not to mention for its feline themes). Without a doubt, it's the Catnip IPA that put this place on the map.

BREWERY

Le Noctem, artisans brasseurs (brewpub)
438 rue du Parvis
Quebec City, QC
G1K 6H8
581 742-7979
noctem.ca

NEARBY BREWERY

La Korrigane
380 rue Dorchester
Quebec City, QC G1K 6A7
418 614-0932
korrigane.ca

WHERE TO TRY THIS BEER

At the brewpub on rue du Parvis. The beer goes down even better on their sunny patio.

WHERE TO BUY THIS BEER

Noctem's beers are sold by the can at several retailers throughout the province and at their other location, Brasserie St-Malo. You can also buy growlers on-site.

WENDAKE TO LIMOILOU

SEE NATURE WITHOUT STEPPING OUTSIDE THE CITY

STARTING POINT	DESTINATION
KABIR KOUBA WATERFALL	NANO CINCO
BEER	**DIFFICULTY**
LIMOICOOL	STRENUOUS
DOG FRIENDLY	**SEASON**
YES, ON LEASH	YEAR-ROUND
FEES	**DURATION**
NO	6 HOURS
MAP REFERENCE	**LENGTH**
AVAILABLE AT QUEBEC CITY TOURIST INFORMATION OFFICES	21.5 KM
HIGHLIGHTS	**ELEVATION CHANGE**
KABIR KOUBA WATERFALL, SAINT-CHARLES RIVER, OLD LIMOILOU	ASCENT: 114 M DESCENT: 223 M

AMERICAN WHEAT PALE ALE

YELLOW, CLOUDY

CITRUS, HOPS

TART, THIRST-QUENCHING, CITRUS

BITTERNESS

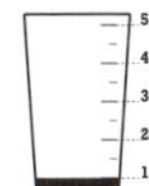

SWEETNESS

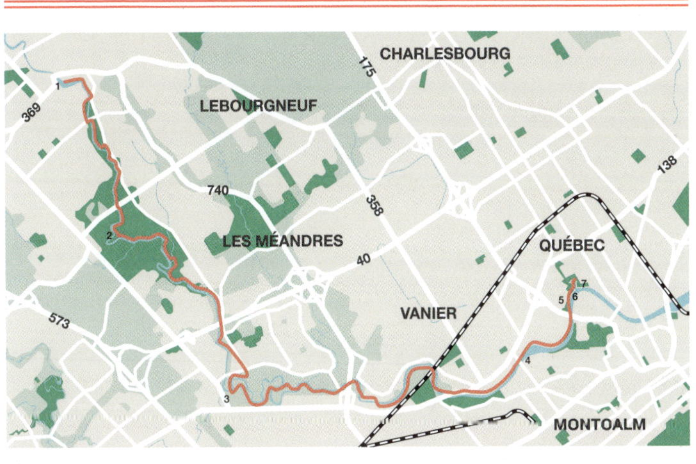

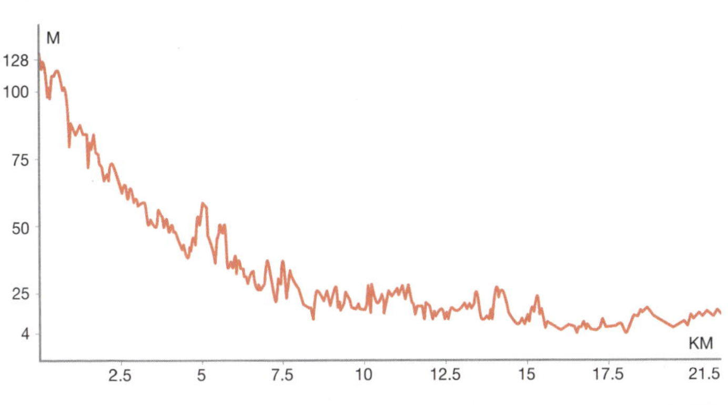

HIKE DESCRIPTION

Hike a section of the Saint-Charles River Linear Park, starting at the Kabir Kouba waterfall, and walk all the way to the charming neighborhood of Limoilou, where you'll chase down a refreshing Limoicool beer.

The Saint-Charles River Linear Park is 32 kilometers long and stretches from Old Quebec to Lake Saint-Charles. The park is divided into 13 sections and today's hike starts in section 10, at the Kabir Kouba waterfall[1] in the village of Wendake, an urban reserve that is home to the Huron-Wendat First Nation.

Along the way, you'll pass through other sections: Chauveau (section 9), l'Estacade (section 8), Parc des Saules (section 7), Duberger (section 5), du Pont de l'Aqueduc (section 4), and des Îlots (section 3). Finally, when you get to section 2, L'Anse-à-Cartier, you'll exit the trail and enter the neighborhood of Limoilou with over 21 kilometers of hiking under your belt.

The best way to track your progress is to watch out for the markers along the trail that tell you how many kilometers are left to go. You can also just note the different areas and follow the directions. Most trail sections are well marked, but it's not always the case. In any event, it's hard to lose your way—just follow the river and you'll end up in town one day! Some trail sections are not accessible in winter (such as l'Estacade and Kabir Kouba waterfall areas), but alternate trails are available to walkers.

So, you're at the access point to the Kabir Kouba waterfall (the name means "river with a thousand detours" in the Wendat language), located already 21 km into the hike (marker 21). From the parking lot, first go right and down the stairs to get a view of the waterfall. Return to the parking lot. The trailhead is on your right. The first part of the journey is interrupted by staircase after staircase going up and down with views out over the waterfall.

Two parks, Chauveau[2] (15 km marker) and des Saules[3] (10 km marker), are great places to stop for a well-deserved snack. You'll also find toilets in no fewer than five places along the way. The same cannot be said for water fountains, so don't forget to take some water with you. You'll pass by several different neighborhoods and settings, including a marsh[4]. Shortly before reaching Cartier-Brébeuf Park, you'll see Dorion-Coulombe house[5], where the Société de la Rivière Saint-Charles, a citizen-driven non-profit organization responsible for the river's sustainable development, is based. Feel free to visit.

Once you're at Cartier-Brébeuf Park[6], stay on the trail, which will take you by the interpretation center, and then follow the bike path back to the river. Keep going and you will go under an overpass. A short time later, you'll see a sign for an access point to 3e Avenue. Go left and

when you get to 3e Avenue[7], turn left and head for 3e Rue, where you will again turn left. Nano Cinco is on your left.

Notes:
You'll have to cross several streets and boulevards. When you do, the trail is always easy to find on the other side.

Other options:
This hike can start at several places, which gives you the flexibility of choosing the distance you're in the mood for. More ambitious hikers might want to start at the Léopold-E.-Beaulieu Ecological Center in section 13, which is a full day's worth of hiking. If for some reason you have to cut your hike short, do the first part and then take public transit to the microbrewery.

TRANSPORTATION

The best way to get to the waterfall is by bus. Take Route 801 to the Charlesbourg terminal. Lines 72 and 75 service this terminal and stop in front of the access point to the waterfall. Get off at the A.-Duchesneau bus stop. The RTC's real-time Nomade app is great for planning trips in the city.

You can also park your car near the Kabir Kouba waterfall, but you'll have to come back by bus or taxi.

TRAIL INFORMATION

Société de la Rivière Saint-Charles
332 Rue Domagaya
Quebec City, QC G1L 5B1
418 691-4710
societerivierestcharles.qc.ca

TOURIST INFORMATION

Bureau d'accueil touristique Tourisme Wendake
10 Place de la Rencontre
Wendake, QC G0A 4V0
418 847-0624
tourismewendake.ca

Tourisme ville de Québec
quebec-cite.com

NANO CINCO

Nano Cinco is what happens when four friends with a shared passion for experimentation (Mathieu Pelletier, Paul Simon, William Berton, and Éloi Paradis-Deschênes) put their minds together. Limoilou is a vibrant neighborhood, and the brewery fits in just nicely, thanks in part to its use of unexpected ingredients. The brewery specializes in brewing IPAs and stouts, as well as thirst-quenching beers and fruity or barrel-aged sours. The beers are brewed in small batches, so they're always made fresh.

BREWERY

Nano Cinco – Brasserie artisanale
236 3e Rue
Quebec City, QC G1L 2S8
581 705-0535
nanocinco.com

NEARBY BREWERIES

La Souche
801 Chemin de la Canardière
Quebec City, QC G1J 2B8
581 742-1144
lasouche.ca

Brasseurs sur demande
1177 Chemin de la Canardière
Quebec City, QC G1J 2C3
581 700-4593
brasseurssurdemande.com

WHERE TO TRY THIS BEER

At the on-site tasting room.

WHERE TO BUY THIS BEER

Alimentation L'impact (incredible selection of craft beers)
1600 4e Avenue
Quebec City, QC G1J 3C3

STONEHAM-ET-TEWKESBURY

WALK ALONG WATERFALLS AND REACH NEW HEIGHTS

STARTING POINT	DESTINATION
STONEHAM MOUNTAIN RESORT	STONEHAM MOUNTAIN RESORT
BEER	**DIFFICULTY**
LIMOILOISE	MODERATE
DOG FRIENDLY	**SEASON**
YES, ON LEASH	YEAR-ROUND
FEES	**DURATION**
NO	3.5 HOURS
MAP REFERENCE	**LENGTH**
AVAILABLE AT RECEPTION	9.5 KM
HIGHLIGHTS	**ELEVATION CHANGE**
MOUNT STONEHAM, VILLAGE OF STONEHAM	ASCENT: 432 M DESCENT: 434 M

ENGLISH PALE ALE

YELLOW, CLOUDY

MALT, FRUIT

SPICY, FRUITY

BITTERNESS

SWEETNESS

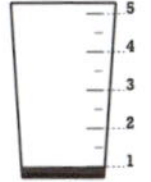

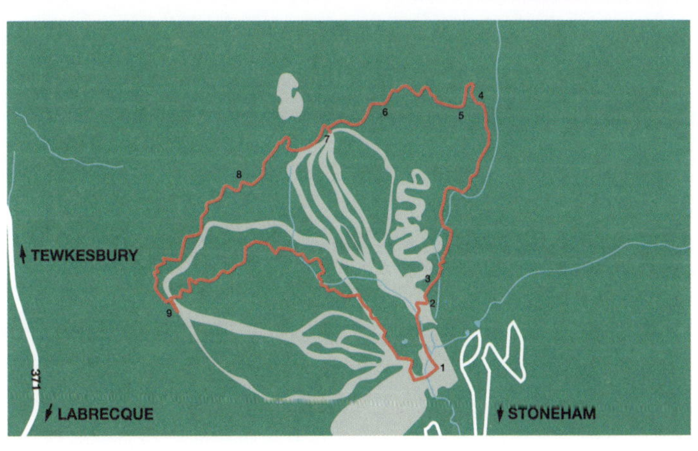

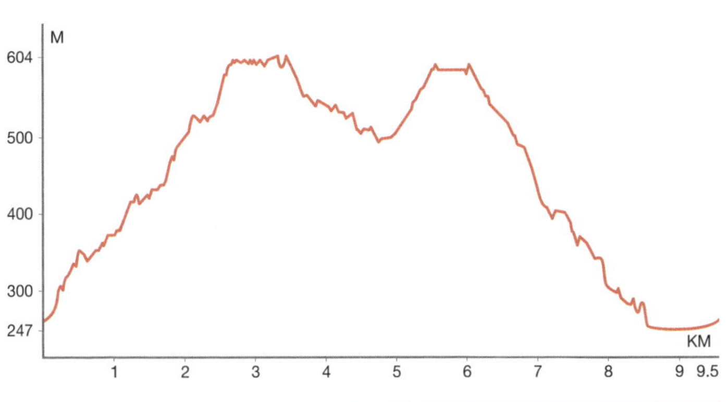

HIKE DESCRIPTION

Offering magnificent views, this hike takes you on a loop starting and ending at the Stoneham Mountain Resort. Afterward, end your day at La Souche Stoneham.

The Stoneham Mountain Resort (Station touristique Stoneham), located 20 minutes from downtown Quebec City, is such a hot spot for winter sports enthusiasts that its summer attractions are often overshadowed. The station actually has two different hikes, one—a 9.5-kilometer loop that incorporates two peaks—is part of Le Sentier national au Québec (National Trail).

The hike starts where the Chemin des Skieurs ends. To get there, from the main parking lot[1] turn right and follow signs for Boucle de la station (at the back of the lot, on your right)[2].

The hike starts with a nice, gentle climb along the pretty Hibou River before crossing a wooden bridge straddling a small waterfall[3]. After this, the trail gradually starts to rise. Keep going straight and when you get to the fork leading toward Sentier du Hibou Nord, continue to follow the signs for Boucle de la station or Station Stoneham.

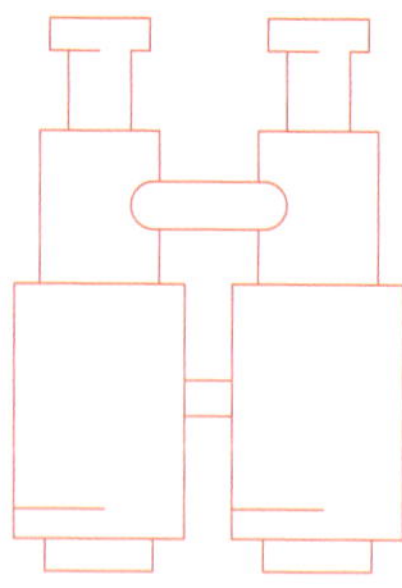

Here the trail gets much steeper, but the reward for your efforts comes quickly in the form of two lookouts[4,5] that offer views of the neighboring mountains and the village of Stoneham. Push on and soon you'll be at the top of the first mountain[6], near the chairlift. This spot offers an uninterrupted view, so soak it in before heading back into the woods to continue your adventure.

By now, most of the uphill climb is behind you, but there's still a bit left to go! The next few kilometers are made up of low-grade ups and downs. This section of the trail takes you through a collection of impressive boulders, gentle streams, and ever-changing vegetation.

You'll come upon a third lookout[7] and, at the second peak, another chairlift. You're now at an elevation of 560 meters, so enjoy the views and give yourself a pat on the back.

Now you may wonder, what is there left to do? Head back down, of course! The descent is a few kilometers of woodland punctuated with brooks, rivers, bridges, and more vistas[8,9]. The end of the trail is marked by an open area.

If you parked in the main parking lot, keep going straight until you get to the entrance on your left, leading behind a building. Climb the stairs, go between the businesses, and head back down.

If you left your car in the second parking lot, go left immediately to get to a paved road. The parking lot is at the end, on the right-hand side. In both parking scenarios, return to the main reception area and head south on Chemin du Hibou. Your microbrewery, La Souche, is only 4.7 kilometers away on your left. When you get there, order yourself a pint of Limoiloise, an English pale ale.

TRANSPORTATION

You can take public transit to Stoneham Mountain Resort. Head to the avenue du Zoo terminal. (Several lines service the stop, such as the

800, 801, and 802. Be sure to check the RTC website for times.) Then take the 23 or 24 (Jacques-Cartier regional municipal county) and get off at the last stop (Chemin du Hibou, Station touristique Stoneham).

If you are driving, you can park at the resort's reception area, do the hike, and hop back in your car to complete the last 4.7 km to La Souche.

TRAIL INFORMATION

Station touristique Stoneham
600 Chemin du Hibou
Stoneham-et-Tewkesbury, QC
G3C 1T3
418 848-2411
ski-stoneham.com/randonnee

TOURIST INFORMATION

Bureau d'accueil touristique de Stoneham (visitor reception)
601 1re avenue
Stoneham-et-Tewkesbury, QC
G0A 4P0
418 848-6377
jacques-cartier.com

Tourisme ville de Québec
quebeccite.com

LA SOUCHE STONEHAM

With university behind him, Antoine Bernatchez, a trained biologist, decided to jump into something he'd dabbled with already: the world of brewing. With the help of a firecracker of a team, he realized his microbrew dreams with La Souche. Firmly embedded in the Limoilou neighborhood since 2012, La Souche opened a second location in Stoneham in 2017. The brewery's woodsy interior is worthy of an old-time Quebec *veillée* (akin to a kitchen party) and fits perfectly with the region. La Souche has a beer for every taste: no one will go away disappointed.

BREWERY

La Souche Stoneham
22 1re avenue
Stoneham-et-Tewkesbury, QC
G3C 0K7
418 848-8529
lasouche.ca

WHERE TO TRY THIS BEER

On-site, in the tasting area and restaurant.

WHERE TO BUY THIS BEER

At the shop adjoining the microbrewery and in several stores throughout the province.

ABITIBI-TÉMISCAMINGUE

ROUYN-NORANDA

AN AREA OF UNIQUE BEAUTY DESIGNED BY GLACIERS

STARTING POINT	DESTINATION
BEAUDRY PARKING LOT	BEAUDRY PARKING LOT
BEER	**DIFFICULTY**
GOSEBUSTER	MODERATE
DOG FRIENDLY	**SEASON**
YES, ON LEASH	YEAR-ROUND
FEES	**DURATION**
NO	4 HOURS
MAP REFERENCE	**LENGTH**
DISPLAYED AT TRAILHEAD	9 KM
HIGHLIGHTS	**ELEVATION CHANGE**
BEAUCHASTEL LAKE, BEAVER DAMS, ERRATIC BOULDERS, 360° VIEW OF SURROUNDING AREA	ASCENT: 300 M DESCENT: 300 M

IMPERIAL GOSE

MURKY, GOLDEN YELLOW

LIME, BRINE

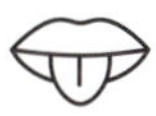

KAFFIR LIME, SEA SALT, CORIANDER

BITTERNESS

SWEETNESS

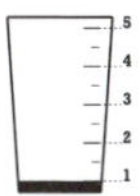

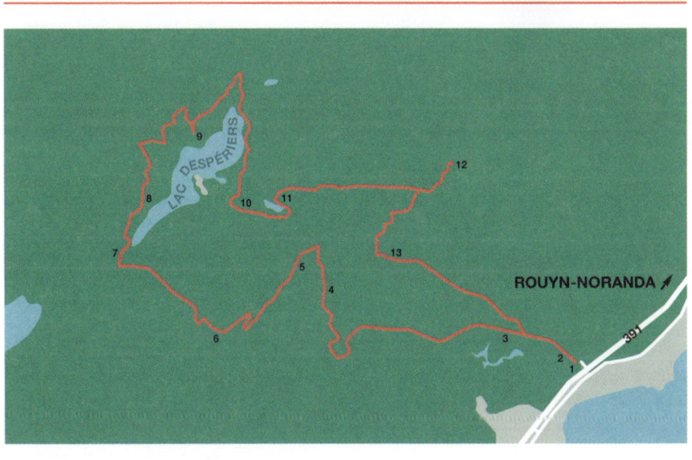

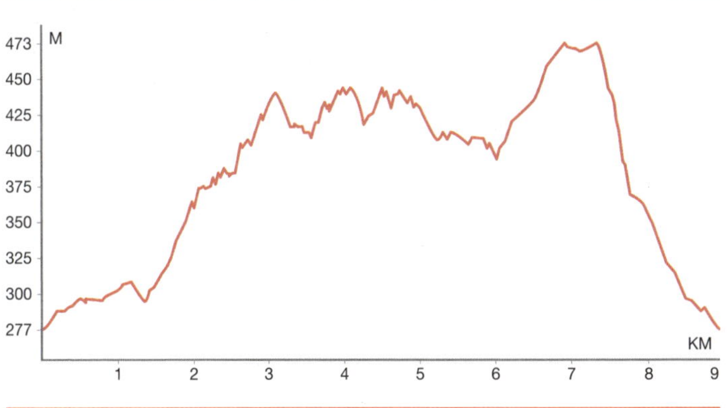

HIKE DESCRIPTION

If you find yourself in Rouyn-Noranda, chances are you've been driving for hours (unless you're a proud and loyal local, in which case you're already there). Well done! It's well worth the journey. You deserve a reward: a hike like no other.

The Kékéko hills (*kékéko* means "sparrowhawk" in the Algonquin language) are located just a few kilometers from the city of Rouyn-Noranda. The massif spans an area of 32 km^2 and is covered in boreal forest typical of the Abitibi region. There are at least 15 marked trails totaling over 40 kilometers, and each one offers awe-inspiring views worthy of this part of Quebec. There are walls created by the movement of glaciers two billion years ago. Beaver dams and rock shelters are common sights. The landscape is dotted with stunning escarpments, erratic boulders, marshes, and lakes of breathtaking beauty.

The recommended hike is a collection of some of the prettier trails, but you can add others and prolong the experience as you see fit. Keep in mind that the trails remain open during hunting season, so caution is highly recommended. Tourisme Abitibi-Témiscamingue has a free trail app called Access 2 Outdoors that can be downloaded to your mobile device.

The hike starts at the Beaudry parking lot[1] of Route 391, about 11 kilometers after exiting the city. The trailhead is well marked but take a moment to familiarize yourself with the map located at the back of the parking lot before setting out.

The first part of the hike follows a road called Petit Chemin Kékéko[2]. Keep going until you reach a fork in the road, in about 400 meters. Then, take the trail on your left, Sentier du Ruisseau[3] (*ruisseau* means "stream"), which runs along a tranquil brook where miniature waterfalls[4] bring the landscape to life.

After about two kilometers, veer left onto Sentier des Remparts[5] (this section is challenging). The view is simply spectacular, with walls made from the sediment left behind by glaciers against a backdrop of panoramic[6] southwestern views of the region. Keep your eyes open—the cliffs are sheer and rockslides are common in the area.

At the end of Sentier des Remparts (1.5 km) you'll find yourself back on Petit Chemin Kékéko. Cross the road to connect with the scenic Sentier Despériers[7] trail, and catch your breath as your eyes feast on the spectacular view extending out over the cliff face. On this trail, you'll discover beaver dams, glacial boulders, a marshland, and a small valley, as well as experience pretty views[8] of Lake Despériers, which the trail wraps around. Make sure to check out the outstanding view near the Virgin Mary[9].

Once again, you'll end up on Petit Chemin Kékéko[10]. Keep left for a few meters and then turn left onto Sentier du Prospecteur[11]. This trail leads to Nid de l'Épervier[12] (meaning "sparrowhawk's nest"), a platform that offers a 360° view of the region. On a clear day, you can even see Mount Chaudron, on the Ontario border, in the distance.

From here, retrace your steps and hang a left at the fork to follow the remainder of Sentier du Prospecteur, which will take you down and over a steep bank back onto Petit Chemin Kékéko[13]. Take a left and you'll eventually arrive back at the parking lot.

From the parking lot, hop back into your vehicle and head left on boulevard Témiscamingue (Route 391). As you enter the city, turn left onto avenue Québec, and then right onto rue Monseigneur-Tessier Ouest. Keep going until you arrive at rue Principale. On the left-hand side is your microbrewery, Le Trèfle Noir (*the black clover/shamrock*), where a well-deserved Gosebuster awaits.

Notes:
If you're feeling adventurous, why not extend the adventure beyond Nid de l'Épervier. Take, for example, Sentier de l'Aventurier (very strenuous) or Sentier du Réflecteur (strenuous), followed by Sentier Panorama, Sentier du Trappeur, and Sentier de l'Orignal. If you feel like hanging around even longer, make a detour through loops 1 and 2. There are lots of options and all of them eventually end up on Petit Chemin Kékéko, which takes you back to your starting point.

TRANSPORTATION

The Rouyn-Noranda bus station is located at 25 avenue Horne. From there, you have to make your own way to the starting point. If you are taking a car to Rouyn-Noranda, park at the Beaudry parking lot on Route 391. It's also fairly easy to find a parking spot in the downtown.

TRAIL INFORMATION

Outdoors Abitibi-Témiscamingue
accesstooutdoors.org

TOURIST INFORMATION

Bureau d'information touristique de Rouyn-Noranda
1675 avenue Larivière
Rouyn-Noranda, QC
J9Y 0G6
tourismerouyn-noranda.ca

Tourisme Abitibi-Témiscamingue
abitibi-temiscamingue.org

LE TRÈFLE NOIR

Le Trèfle Noir opened its doors in 2009 and is the first craft brewery in Abitibi-Témiscamingue to have a tasting room on-site. Alexandre Groulx and his partner Mireille Bournival are the architects of the project. Alexandre was born in Victoriaville and only came to Rouyn-Noranda to finish a degree in multimedia design. Mireille is from the area and picked up a considerable amount of experience in the food service industry when she was a student. Alexandre and his team enjoy experimenting with different beers and draw inspiration from the trails blazed by others.

BREWERY

Le Trèfle Noir
145 avenue Principale
Rouyn-Noranda, QC
J9X 4P3
819 762-6611

WHERE TO TRY THIS BEER

At the brewery.

WHERE TO BUY THIS BEER

Chez Gibb Centre-Ville (specialty store)
60A avenue Principale
Rouyn-Noranda, QC
J9X 4P2

BAS-SAINT-LAURENT

SAINT-ANDRÉ-DE-KAMOURASKA

FROM MONADNOCK HIGHS TO TIDAL FLAT LOWS

STARTING POINT	DESTINATION
SEBKA RECEPTION AREA	TÊTE D'ALLUMETTE MICROBREWERY
BEER	**DIFFICULTY**
ŒIL DU MOUTON	MODERATE
DOG FRIENDLY	**SEASON**
NO	MID-MAY TO MID-OCTOBER
FEES	**DURATION**
YES, PAY AT SEBKA RECEPTION	2 HOURS
MAP REFERENCE	**LENGTH**
AVAILABLE AT SEBKA VISITOR CENTER	6.9 KM
HIGHLIGHTS	**ELEVATION CHANGE**
ST. LAWRENCE RIVER, SANDBANKS, MONADNOCKS	ASCENT: 195 M DESCENT: 212 M

NORWEGIAN VOSSAØL

AMBER, CLOUDY

CARAMEL, JAM, SMOKY, CANDIED ORANGE

BARLEY SUGAR,CLOVES, STRAWBERRIES, FIR, PEAT

BITTERNESS

SWEETNESS

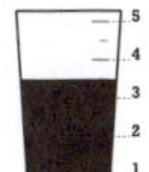

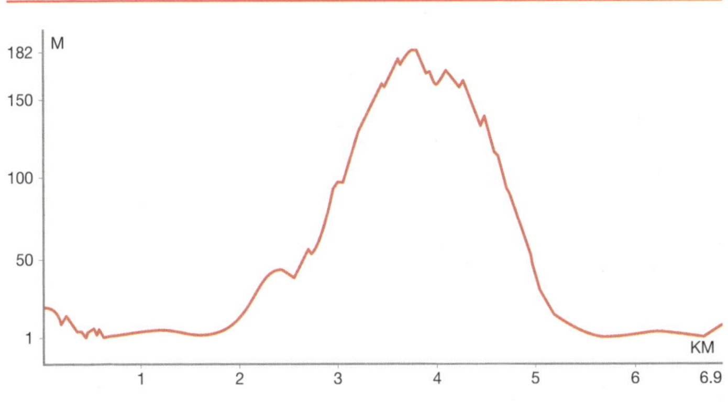

HIKE DESCRIPTION

High up or down low, there's always a great view on this hike. Breathe in the air of the salt marsh, let your gaze wander, and get acquainted with Kamouraska over a good Norwegian beer.

Saint-André-de-Kamouraska is situated in a very desirable area. At the crossroads of several tourist routes, the village is nestled between the sandbanks of the St. Lawrence River and the Monadnocks (*isolated mountain* in the Abenaki language), which are hills made of quartzite, typical of this region.

This hike starts at the visitor center of the Société d'écologie de la batture du Kamouraska (SEBKA)[1], a non-profit organization created to protect the region's natural environment. This is where you will pay your admission fee.

From the visitor center, head east on Sentier de la Batture[3], which runs along a marsh and connects the park's two sectors. You'll pass behind your end destination, a microbrewery named Tête d'Allumette[7], but don't succumb to the urge to head for the patio just yet! Keep going for another 1.4 kilometers, until you get to the next parking lot in the Amphithéâtre sector[4].

Cross the parking lot and Route 132. This is the starting point for the Amphithéâtre sector trails, and it's easy to find. Your mission today is to complete the Boucle des Écoliers (the Schoolchildren's Loop), a short trail that will bring you to the very top of the Monadnock. There, you'll

be treated to a 360° view of the area. There's nothing complicated about this hike; just follow the signs as you make your way around the loop.

The Boucle des Écoliers starts on the edge of a field before gently veering left into the woods. The first kilometer is fairly easy.

Soon after the terrain gets trickier, but you won't have to wait long to be rewarded. There are two viewpoints[5] and a lookout[6] from which you can cast your gaze over the majestic St. Lawrence River and admire the cluster of islands offshore. There's also a great view of the surrounding landscape to enjoy. If you're lucky, you might spot climbers scaling the rock face, the likes of which is found nowhere else. On a clear day, the eye can see as far as Tadoussac, La Malbaie, and Pointe-au-Pic!

When you've completed the loop, cut back across Route 132 and the parking lot, and then follow Sentier de la Batture along the river until you reach the microbrewery. Pick a spot on the patio and quench your thirst with an Œil du Mouton (Sheep's Eye), an exotic, typically Norwegian brew—Vossaøl—that is made in partnership with the authors of the blog *Les Coureurs des Boires*. You won't forget this beer, nor the décor, which is considered one of the finest among all Quebec microbreweries.

Other options:
Those with a little more ambition could start with the Sentier Panoramique[2]. Head left from the reception area before embarking on the hike described above.

TRANSPORTATION

It's virtually impossible to get to this microbrewery without a car. Park at the SEBKA visitor center or the parking lot in the Amphithéâtre section, located 1.4 kilometers away along Route 132.

TRAIL INFORMATION

Société d'écologie de la batture du Kamouraska (SEBKA)
273 Route 132 Ouest
Saint-André-de-Kamouraska, QC
G0L 2H0
sebka.ca

TOURIST INFORMATION

Maison touristique régionale du Bas-Saint-Laurent
10, Route du Quai
La Pocatière, QC
G0R 1Z0
1 888 856-5040
tourismekamouraska.com

Tourisme Bas-Saint-Laurent
bassaintlaurent.ca

TÊTE D'ALLUMETTE

Tête d'Allumette (Matchstick Head) is a story of perseverance, passion, and purpose in the face of adversity. Martin Desautels and Élodie Fortin saw their first endeavor, La Camarine—a food co-op where they had plans to brew their own beers—go up in flames one morning just before the brew equipment was supposed to arrive. In 2013, they opened Tête d'Allumette in an old family home on the river's edge and it is, by design, a place for people to come together.

With the desire to set himself apart and put his own stamp on things, Martin had the bold, if not crazy, idea to go down the path of wood-fired brewing. Marrying modern technology with ancestral brew techniques, his method gives his products a taste you'll find nowhere else. His lightbulb moment came to him during a trip to Europe, more precisely during a visit to the Caracole brewery in Belgium (check out Caracole in the Belgian edition of the Beer Hiking series!).

BREWERY

Microbrasserie Tête d'Allumette
265 route 132
Saint-André-de-Kamouraska, QC
G0L 2H0
418 493-2222
tetedallumette.com

WHERE TO TRY THIS BEER

Right on-site. On the patio is even better!

WHERE TO BUY THIS BEER

At the on-site shop.

EASTERN TOWNSHIPS

BROMONT

A HILLY VIEW FROM MOUNT HORIZON

STARTING POINT	DESTINATION
RUE PIERRE-BELLEFLEUR	BROUEMONT
BEER	DIFFICULTY
DOWN UNDER DOUBLE IPA	MODERATE
DOG FRIENDLY	SEASON
YES, ON LEASH	YEAR-ROUND
FEES	DURATION
YES (FREE FOR RESIDENTS)	4 HOURS
MAP REFERENCE	LENGTH
AVAILABLE AT BROMONT VISITOR CENTER AND RÉSEAU DU MONT BERTHIER	10.6 KM
HIGHLIGHTS	ELEVATION CHANGE
MOUNT HORIZON, VIEW OF HILLS	ASCENT: 398 M DESCENT: 393 M

DOUBLE DRY HOPPED NEW ENGLAND IPA

BRIGHT YELLOW, HAZY

TROPICAL FRUIT, PEACH

TROPICAL FRUIT, HOPPY, SILKY

BITTERNESS

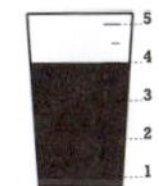

SWEETNESS

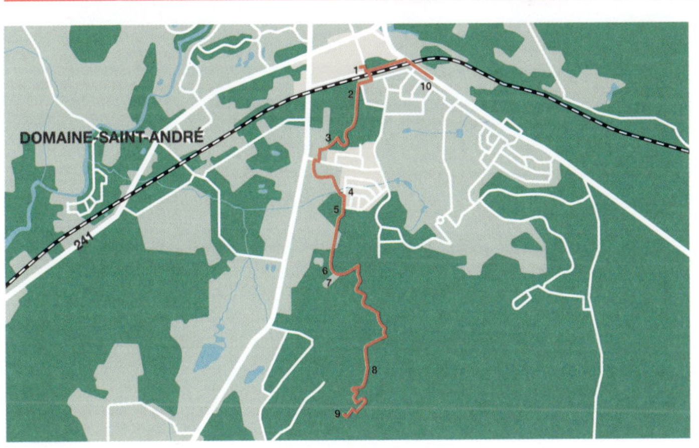

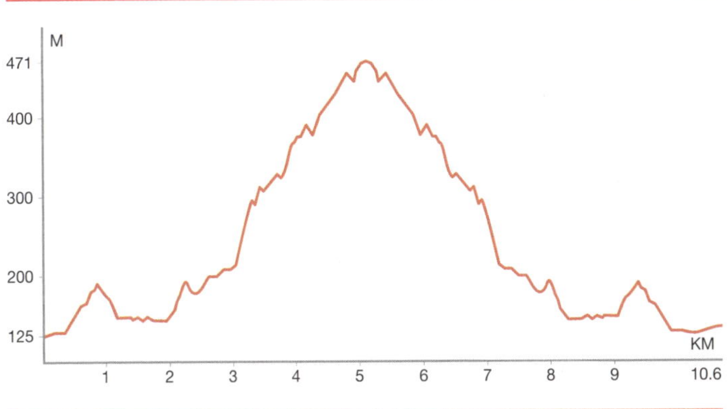

HIKE DESCRIPTION

When people visit the Eastern Townships (Cantons de l'Est), they have one goal in mind: explore the area's rolling landscapes. This is exactly what's in store for you on the trails of Bromont. You will head for the height of Mount Horizon before coming back down to Earth where a delicious beer awaits you.

The journey begins on the Mount Berthier trail network (Réseau du Mont Berthier) on rue Pierre-Bellefleur behind the stadium (for winter hiking, see the notes section below for detours). With your back turned to the sports facilities, locate the bike path and take it. Shortly thereafter, turn right in the direction of the railroad[1] and cross it to get to the beginning of Sentier B1 (Balade)[2] along the roadside (this trail is part of the Mount Berthier network). Take a right and immediately enter the woods. Follow the signs for B1.

At the fork, turn right and follow a section of Sentier B2 (Boucle)[3]. This will take you out of the woods and into a wooded residential neighborhood where eventually you will exit onto rue d'Iberville[4]. Turn right onto rue d'Iberville. When you get to the end, you will head back into the woods.

You will have three options: go left, go straight, or go right. Go right and head into Parc des Sommets, a park within the mountain network (Réseau de la montagne), on Sentier C2 (Cantons)[5]. Your mission is to reach Sentier C13 (Coulée douce)[6], a climb that winds its way through the trees for 1.4 kilometers. This trail is also used by mountain bikers, so please be careful.

Next, take Sentier C14 (Divine)[8]. Follow the signs to the summit of Mount Horizon[9].

Once you've reached the top, enjoy the view of the Montérégie mountains in the distance. To get back down the mountain, retrace your steps. Just before reaching your starting point, take the trail running alongside the railroad on the right, as far as boulevard Bromont. The Brouemont brewery[10] is on your right, and it's time to reward yourself with a nice New England-inspired IPA.

Notes:
Bromont is part of the administrative region of Montérégie, but it is included in the Eastern Townships section from a touristic standpoint.

Other options:
The Coulée Douce trail is closed to hikers during the winter but check with Les Amis des sentiers de Bromont (friends of the Bromont trails) for other routes.

The area has no shortage of trails that can be pieced together to extend your hike. For example, Sentier C1 (Ceinture)[7] is a 15 km loop around the mountain; and C3 and C4 go to the top of Mont Bernard.

TRANSPORTATION

If you are coming by car, park behind the Bromont stadium on rue Pierre-Bellefleur. There are coaches from other towns that stop in Bromont. Get off at the Shefford corner store, located about 400 meters from where the hike starts.

TRAIL INFORMATION

Parc des Sommets
parcdessommets.com

TOURIST INFORMATION

Bureau d'accueil touristique de Bromont (visitor center)
15 boulevard de Bromont
Bromont, QC
J2L 2K4
450 534-2006
tourismebromont.com

Tourisme Cantons-de-l'Est
easterntownships.org

LE BROUEMONT

Diane Moreau and Patrick Dunnigan traveled the globe before finally settling down in Bromont, a city nestled in the beautiful Eastern Townships region. Having already owned a microbrewery (which unfortunately burned down), this athletic couple noticed that Bromont lacked a place for friends to gather for après-ski (or après-hike) over some quality beers.

So, in 2004, the microbrewery Le Brouemont, the first of its kind in Bromont, opened its doors. Patrick and Alexandre Duchesne, brewmaster and brewer, respectively, are responsible for coming up with these brews that never fail to impress.

BREWERY

Le Brouemont
107 boulevard de Bromont
Bromont, QC
J2L 2K7
lebrouement.com

WHERE TO TRY THIS BEER

Right on-site, at the restaurant/pub associated with the brewery.

WHERE TO BUY THIS BEER

You can take away a growler of your favorite beer.

SUTTON

FROM THE VILLAGE TO THE WITCHES' CAULDRON

STARTING POINT	DESTINATION
RUE HIGHLAND	À L'ABORDAGE
BEER	**DIFFICULTY**
GOLDEN ALE	EASY
DOG FRIENDLY	**SEASON**
YES, ON LEASH	YEAR-ROUND
FEES	**DURATION**
NO	3 HOURS
MAP REFERENCE	**LENGTH**
AVAILABLE AT SUTTON VISITOR INFORMATION CENTER	10.4 KM
HIGHLIGHTS	**ELEVATION CHANGE**
PICTURESQUE VILLAGE OF SUTTON, WITCHES' CAULDRON	ASCENT: 192 M DESCENT: 220 M

BRITISH-INSPIRED BLONDE ALE

GOLDEN, CLEAR

GRAIN, HINTS OF GRASS

GRAIN, HINTS OF GRASS, HOPS

BITTERNESS

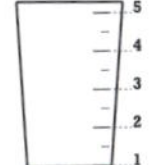

SWEETNESS

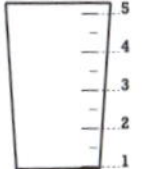

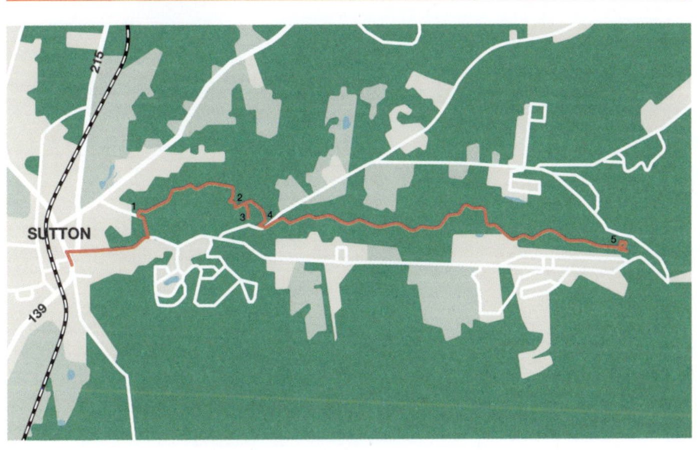

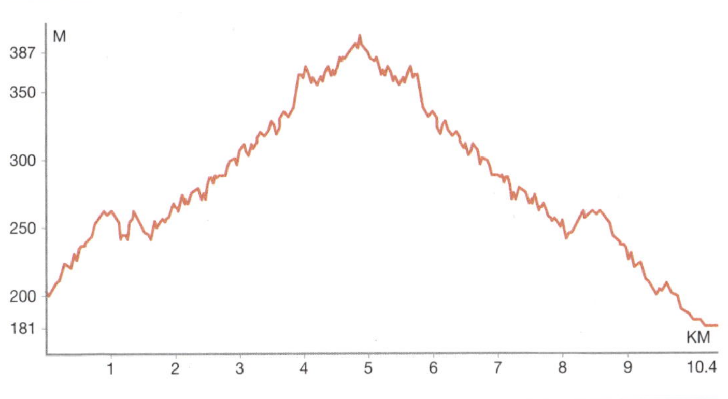

HIKE DESCRIPTION

This hike goes from village to mountain. Along the way, dip your toes in the Marmite aux Sorcières (Witches' Cauldron) before wetting your whistle with a pint of pale ale.

The village of Sutton (a regional county municipality of Brome-Missisquoi) is located in the heart of the Eastern Townships. The village is a true gem when it comes to outdoor activities: you'll find suspended bike riding, skiing, snowshoeing, kayaking, and hiking. This place is a must-see for anyone who appreciates nature, charming villages, and culture.

Take Sentier Village-Montagne, a trail connecting—you guessed it!—the village to the mountain. The trail starts in the very heart of Sutton and follows a straight line to the Marmite aux Sorcières, five kilometers away (6 km if you leave from the village). It ties in with Sutton's natural environment park (Parc d'environnement naturel de Sutton [PENS]), which alone contains over 50 km of trails leading to the Sutton mountains.

The starting point is rue Highland[1], about 10 minutes away from the village center. To get there from the visitor center, head right onto rue Principale Sud, turn right onto Maple, and then on the second street, Highland, turn left. The trailhead is about 200 meters away on your right.

From the trailhead, all you have to do is follow the yellow squares. The trail is well marked the entire way, so there's no chance of getting lost.

In no time at all, you'll be following the river. Cross the wooden platform[2] on your right. Stop and listen to the sounds around you: the river, the birds, the rustling of leaves. Hard to believe you're not far from a busy road! A little further, on your right, you'll see a set of stone stairs[3] leading down to the river. Go ahead—you'll find it most refreshing!

Two and a half kilometers in, cross Chemin Poissant[4] and then keep going through the woods and along the river, which is now on your left. There'll be a few muddy spots and places where you'll have to cross a stream.

Finally, a gentle rise in the trail brings you to an elevation of 379 meters. There, you can enjoy a high-angle view of the Marmite aux Sorcières[5] from an observation deck. The little staircase to your left is there for a reason, so go ahead and take it! The big rocks at the bottom are a great place for a picnic and, while you're there, why not go for a dip in the river? The pools located between two waterfalls are a great choice. So, just what is the Marmite aux Sorcières? This "witches' cauldron" is actually a geological oddity, a series of small pools within the river that, strangely, look like Scandinavian baths.

After this well-deserved break, retrace your steps to where the trail started. Then go left on Highland, right onto Maple, and then left again on rue Principale.

Your microbrewery, À l'Abordage, is situated in the heart of the village. Try the Golden Ale and also explore their beer menu, as it offers a range of high-quality brews. If you feel like spoiling yourself, ask for a Dans les Nuages (In the Clouds), too!

Other options:
The area around Sutton has no shortage of hiking options. Explore what PENS has to offer and let the 6 km Round Top Trail and the arduous 13.8 km loop Boucle des Crêtes blow your mind.

TRANSPORTATION

The Sutton bus station is located at 28 rue Principale, north of rue Maple (therefore you'll have to go left from the station to connect with Maple). If you are arriving in Sutton by car, please know that it is relatively easy to park along the village's streets. Pay attention to the signs and the times when parking is permitted. Aim for the vicinity of the visitor center so you are in the heart of the village.

TRAIL INFORMATION

Parc d'environnement naturel de Sutton
parcsutton.com

TOURIST INFORMATION

Bureau d'accueil touristique de Sutton (visitor center)
27, rue Principale Nord
Sutton, QC
J0E 2K0
450 538-8455
tourismesutton.ca

Tourisme Cantons-de-l'Est
easterntownships.org

À L'ABORDAGE

À L'Abordage came to be thanks to a pair of local athletes, brewer Cédrik Poitras and his partner Dominique Miville-Deschênes. The couple were already amateur brewers when, as students in Montreal, they had an opportunity to learn from professionals. Their dream? To go back home, open their own microbrewery, and start a family. In 2015, they opened a brewery in the heart of picturesque Sutton, in a building dating back to 1843, where they have been making beers ever since. Their beers, mostly of the English and American variety, can be enjoyed on-site after a long day of skiing or likewise, to cap off a day of hiking!

BREWERY

À L'Abordage
10 rue Principale Sud
Sutton, QC
J0E 2K0
450 538-8338
alabordage.beer

NEARBY BREWERY

Auberge Sutton Brouërie
27 rue Principale Sud
Sutton, QC
J0E 2K0
450 538-0005
aubergesuttonbrouerie.com

WHERE TO TRY THIS BEER

Directly on-site.

WHERE TO BUY THIS BEER

Some beers can be purchased on-site.

ORFORD

A FOREST STROLL IN THE HEART OF THE TOWNSHIPS

STARTING POINT	DESTINATION
CENTRE DE DÉCOUVERTE ET DE SERVICES LE CERISIER	CENTRE DE DÉCOUVERTE ET DE SERVICES LE CERISIER
BEER	**DIFFICULTY**
PIC AUX CORBEAUX	MODERATE
DOG FRIENDLY	**SEASON**
NO	YEAR-ROUND
FEES	**DURATION**
YES, SÉPAQ RATES APPLY	3 HOURS
MAP REFERENCE	**LENGTH**
AVAILABLE AT RECEPTION, SÉPAQ MONT-ORFORD	8.3 KM
HIGHLIGHTS	**ELEVATION CHANGE**
VILLAGE OF ORFORD, COLLINE DE LA SERPENTINE, VIEW OF THE EASTERN TOWNSHIPS, ÉTANG AUX CERISES	ASCENT: 230 M DESCENT: 230 M

COFFEE STOUT

BLACK, HAZY

ROASTED COFFEE

ROASTED COFFEE, SMOOTH, CREAMY

BITTERNESS

SWEETNESS

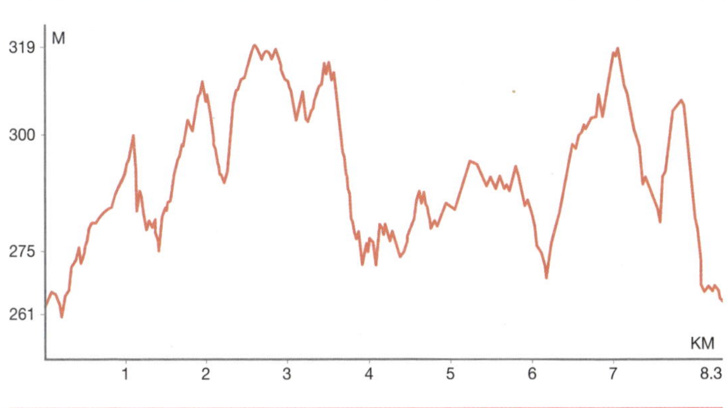

HIKE DESCRIPTION

Walk around Étang aux cerises (Cherry Pond) and get a hilltop view of your surroundings from Colline de la serpentine. And then finish your excursion in the village at Canton Brasse (a fun play on words that sounds like *quand on brasse*, which means "when one brews").

Quebec's Mount Orford provincial park is a go-to place for winter-sport enthusiasts, but it also has something for those who prefer summer, too! Here, you will find some of the best views in the Eastern Townships. The setting is well stocked in mature trees, three-quarters of which are sugar maples—just imagine what it looks like in the fall!

It's not beer time quite yet, so begin your journey around the pond with two trails: Sentier du Pékan and Sentier du Lynx. You'll find the starting point behind the Centre de découverte et de services Le Cerisier[1] the discovery and service center named after cherries, like the pond. The center is located in the Lac-Stukely sector.

For the first part of the hike, follow the signs (yellow and brown squares that display symbols for hiking and snowshoeing) for Sentier du Pékan[2]. It won't take long for this somewhat bumpy trail, with stumps and roots underfoot, to turn into a climb. Keep your eyes on the signs. Because the trail intersects with mountain-bike trails, it's easy to get distracted.

After about a kilometer, you'll come upon Le Vieux-Camp[3], a shelter with toilets. A little further and you will have the option to turn right and take Sentier de la Serpentine[4], a straight, 300-meter ascent up a hill of the same name. The steep climb is worth your while, as it's one of the only points on this hike with a view down below.

After you've descended and are back on Sentier du Pékan, take a left and follow the signs marked "10." In no time, you will be on a two-way path. At the next fork, take another left and when you reach the road, cross it. This trail quickly leads to another refuge, Le Castor[5], where Sentier du Pékan officially ends. Now's a good time to take a break and go to the bathroom.

From here, continue your journey around the pond, this time on Sentier du Lynx[6]. This trail follows the road and takes you back to the discovery and service center.

When you're back where you started, jump in your car and, in five minutes flat, you'll be at the microbrewery Canton Brasse ordering the Pic aux Corbeaux coffee stout.

TRANSPORTATION

The distance between the starting point and the microbrewery is about 2.5 kilometers. From the village, you can get there and back on foot, but bear in mind it involves walking along a busy road, not ideal for pedestrians. This is only to be taken if you promise to be extra cautious. If you do decide to set out from the village, leave your car at Rivière-aux-Cerises Park.

If you take your car to the trailhead, leave it in the parking lot of the Mount Orford Park (at the discovery and service center) of the Lac-Stukely sector.

You can also catch a bus to Orford from certain towns and cities, in which case you'll get dropped off just over five kilometers from Mount Orford.

TRAIL INFORMATION

Parc national du Mont-Orford
819 843-9855
sepaq.com/pq/mor

TOURIST INFORMATION

Bureau d'information touristique Memphrémagog
2911 Chemin Milletta
Magog, QC
J1X 0R4
819 843-2744
tourisme-memphremagog.com

Tourisme Cantons-de-L'Est
easterntownships.org

CANTON BRASSE

It was a passion for good beer and a burning desire to do what they love that led Nicolas and Hugo into the world of brewing—with some help from Nicolas' dad Claude, a born entrepreneur. Situated in the center of the village, the brewery has stolen the hearts of locals, outdoor enthusiasts, and hikers and skiers returning from the mountains. With its warm and friendly ambiance, the brewery offers a large variety of products that range from the classics to innovations you'll find nowhere else.

BREWERY

Canton Brasse
2267 Chemin du Parc
Orford, QC
J1X 7A2
819 868-2165
cantonbrasse.com

WHERE TO TRY THIS BEER

Directly on-site.

WHERE TO BUY THIS BEER

Some beers can be purchased on-site.

COATICOOK

STROLL THROUGH A GLACIER-CARVED CANYON

STARTING POINT	DESTINATION
PARC DE LA GORGE DE COATICOOK	MICROBRASSERIE DE COATICOOK
BEER	**DIFFICULTY**
L'ABYSSE DE LA GORGE	MODERATE
DOG FRIENDLY	**SEASON**
YES, ON LEASH	YEAR-ROUND
FEES	**DURATION**
YES, PAY AT RECEPTION	3.5 HOURS
MAP REFERENCE	**LENGTH**
AVAILABLE AT PARK RECEPTION	8 KM
HIGHLIGHTS	**ELEVATION CHANGE**
SUSPENDED FOOTBRIDGE, COATICOOK GORGE CANYON, WATERFALLS, CAVE	ASCENT: 156 M DESCENT: 188 M

OAT STOUT

BLACK

CHOCOLATE, COFFEE

DARK CHOCOLATE, ESPRESSO

BITTERNESS SWEETNESS

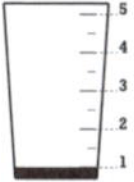

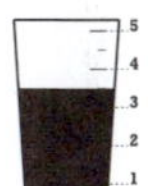

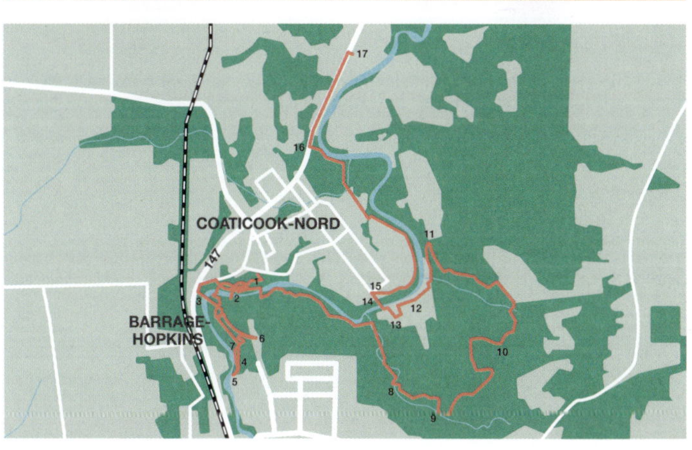

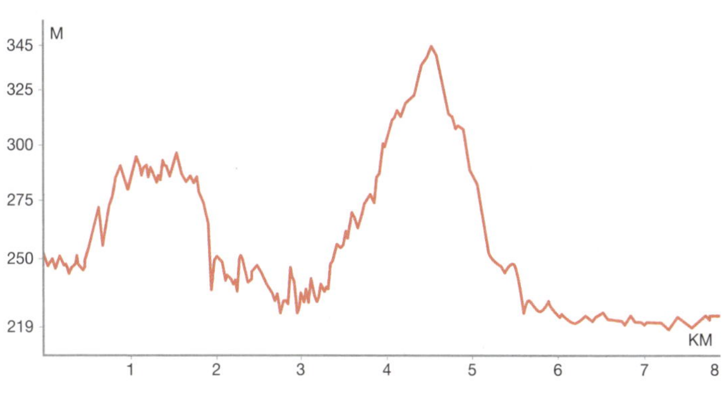

HIKE DESCRIPTION

Put your fear of heights to the test as you cross one of the world's longest suspension bridges in Parc de la Gorge de Coaticook, a park named for the town's canyon. Then reward yourself with a beer at Microbrasserie de Coaticook. In winter, the trails can be done on snowshoe but are not exactly as described in this book. Inquire before setting out.

It is believed Coaticook's gorge, which is 750 meters long and, in places, 50 meters deep, was formed by a melting glacier. The park is famous for its 169-meter suspension bridge, which may well be the longest pedestrian suspension bridge in North America.

The park has 16 kilometers of trails divided into three circuits: Sentier de la Gorge (3.5 km), Sentier de la Montagne (3–4 km), and Sentier Tillotson (8.5 km). While most visitors stick to Sentier de la Gorge, my recommendation is to string the first two together (you can add on the third if you're really determined).

The hike starts at the reception[1] on rue Michaud. This first trail gets a lot of traffic and is so well marked it would be almost ridiculous to give you a step-by-step description. Just follow the signs for Sentier de la Gorge, plain and simple.

There are a number of interesting things to see throughout this trail: a lookout[2], a famous suspension bridge[3], a small cave[4], a hydroelectric plant[5], a seven-story observation tower[6], and several footbridges[7] clinging to the sides of a rocky ravine that will test your fear of heights.

The good thing about this first part of the hike is that it packs a lot of fun things into a short period of time. There's nothing challenging about this section, apart from a good calf workout (thank you, stairs!).

When you're back at the starting point, follow the signs for Sentier de la Montagne. You didn't think you'd be going to the microbrewery after just 3.5 kilometers, did you? A two-lane road running alongside the river takes you through a campground, after which you'll find the trail's true starting point[8]. Here, too, the terrain is nothing complicated, but there is a series of decent up-and-down sections. Follow the river[9], with its gorgeous little waterfalls. Here you can venture out onto the rocks for a snack—zenitude guaranteed—before ducking back into the woods.

At about the halfway point, you'll come upon another observation tower[10]. (Notice the smile on your face as you climb its seven stories.)

The next part of the hike brings you back into a coniferous forest that gradually becomes more deciduous.

Next, you'll come upon a field. There you'll follow a little road until the signs lead you back, one last time, into the woods on your left.

From the woods, there's a long descent back to the road you started on[11], which leads right back to the campground[12].

When you get to the campground, head for the reception area[13] and cross the old covered bridge[14]. On your right, take the Axe Nord bike path[15] that cuts across an open area and along the forest edge. You'll end up on a road[16], rue Child, after passing by a sport facility. Cross the street and keep going on the bike path toward the right.

You'll quickly reach the parking lot for the Laiterie de Coaticook, one of Quebec's largest ice cream producers. Your microbrewery, Microbrasserie de Coaticook[17], is just across the street, where the perfect end to the day, an astonishingly refreshing Abysse de la Gorge stout, awaits.

TRANSPORTATION

Apart from rare, local exceptions, the town of Coaticook is not regularly serviced by public transit. If you arrive in Coaticook by car, park at the canyon park, Parc de la Gorge de Coaticook.

TRAIL INFORMATION

Parc de la Gorge de Coaticook
135 rue Michaud
Coaticook, QC
J1A 2A4
1 888 524-6743
gorgedecoaticook.qc.ca

TOURIST INFORMATION

Bureau d'accueil touristique de Coaticook
137 rue Michaud
Coaticook, QC
J1A 1A9
819 849-6669
tourismecoaticook.ca

Tourisme Cantons-de-l'Est
easterntownships.org

MICROBRASSERIE DE COATICOOK

Réjean Corbeil, brewer, and Barry Hull opened the microbrewery in 2013. A few years later, Barry's daughter, Sarah Jolicœur-Hull, joined them and brought her strong background in communications and marketing to her role as general manager.

The team is committed to authenticity, which they achieve by serving up palate-pleasing unfiltered beers. The place is also home to a restaurant where pub-style food, starring local products, is on offer. Over 10 beers are brewed on-site all year long. That number doesn't include brews inspired and limited by the availability of seasonal products, such as raspberries, maple syrup, and cranberries.

BREWERY

Microbrasserie de Coaticook
1007 rue Child
Coaticook, QC
J1A 2S5
819 804-1234
microbrasseriecoaticook.ca

WHERE TO TRY THIS BEER

At the brewery.

WHERE TO BUY THIS BEER

At the shop annexed to the microbrewery and at several retail outlets throughout Quebec.

HAM-SUD AND HAM-NORD

SHORT HIKE, SPECTACULAR VIEW

STARTING POINT	DESTINATION
RECEPTION, PARC RÉGIONAL DU MONT-HAM	RECEPTION, PARC RÉGIONAL DU MONT-HAM
BEER	**DIFFICULTY**
AVOUÈNE DU GOSFORD	MODERATE TO STRENUOUS
DOG FRIENDLY	**SEASON**
NO, EXCEPT ON CERTAIN DATES	YEAR-ROUND
FEES	**DURATION**
YES, PAY AT RECEPTION OR ONLINE	3 HOURS
MAP REFERENCE	**LENGTH**
AVAILABLE AT VISITOR CENTER	4.8 KM
HIGHLIGHTS	**ELEVATION CHANGE**
WEEPING ROCK, 360° VIEW OF EASTERN TOWNSHIPS AND CENTRE-DU-QUÉBEC REGION	ASCENT: 340 M DESCENT: 340 M

FARMHOUSE ALE

STRAW-YELLOW, CLOUDY

FRUIT, PEPPERS, CANDIED CITRUS

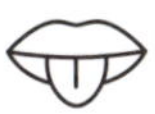

CANDIED CITRUS, SPICES, FRUIT

BITTERNESS

SWEETNESS

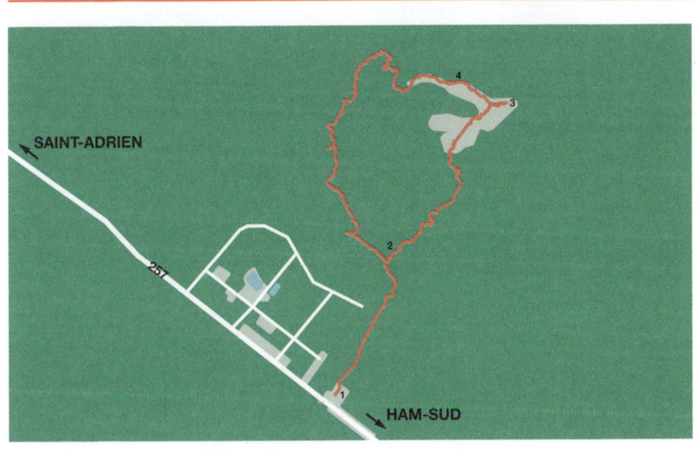

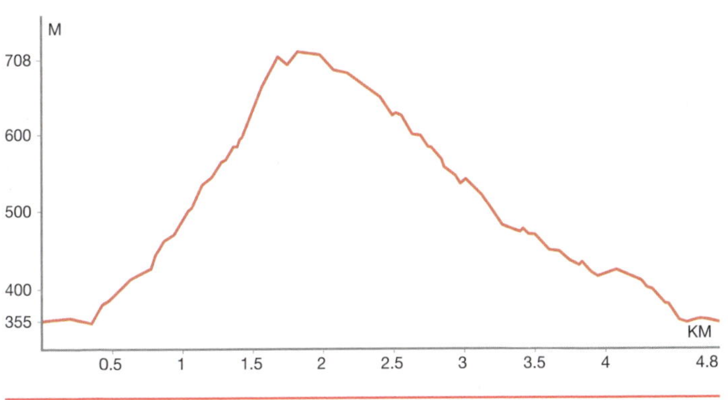

HIKE DESCRIPTION

The Parc régional du Mont-Ham (Mount Ham Regional Park) is located in Ham-Sud, in the regional county municipality of Les Sources. It boasts 18 kilometers of trails accessible year-round and ranging from moderate to strenuous.

Formed more than 500 million years ago by continental drift and reaching heights of 713 meters, Mount Ham is part of the Appalachian Plateau. With a certain majesty, Mount Ham looks out over the surrounding valleys, and its summit offers a panoramic view of fields and forests.

Several trail combinations make it possible to get to the peak. The recommended one is a bit of a workout, but it's also the most impressive, while remaining relatively accessible and short (less than 5 kilometers). In my opinion, the trail is a destination by itself: there's nothing but beauty all around, from start to finish, and it strikes a perfect effort/reward balance.

The hike starts behind the reception building[1]. Take the Intrépide Trail[2], which is rated very strenuous, as you will see, but rest assured, most of it is moderate. Toward the end, there are ropes to help you finish your climb, so make sure you have good footwear and take your time. During my hike, there were people of various ages, including children, doing it. The hike might be a little intimidating for a first-time hiker, but it can definitely be done by anyone with a smidge of motivation (say, a good, end-of-hike beer) and in good physical condition.

The Intrépide Trail, which is barely 1.9 kilometers, is very well marked right to the top. You'll need a solid hour to hike it. The first section is relatively easy, with a slight incline. There are makeshift wooden footbridges, rustic stairs, and boulders along the way. When you get to the Roche pleureuse (Weeping Rock), take a left and keep following the signs to the top.

The last few hundred meters might give you a harder time, but (pinkie swear) the effort is worth it, and you won't regret a thing. You'll pass a series of rocky promontories where you might need to use your hands from time to time. Ropes have been installed to make the climb a little easier.

My advice is to allot some time to linger at the top[3]. Let your eyes wander. Explore. Breathe. You might consider eating here too! Don't forget to check out Awdowinno, a statue with a name that means "warrior" in the Abenaki language.

When you're finished getting your thrill, get ready for the journey back. Whenever possible, a different return route is suggested, so find Panoramique Trail[4] (you'll have no trouble finding the signs at the summit). This moderate-level trail winds down around the mountain over a distance of 2.1 kilometers before ending at the reception area. The last part of the trail will look familiar, and that's because you took it at the beginning of the hike.

Now, head for Ham-Nord and the brewery farm called La Grange Pardue. Order yourself an Avouène du Gosford (*avouène* reflects a local pronunciation of *avoine*, meaning "oats").

Notes:
Mount Ham, located in Ham-Sud, is part of the Eastern Townships. However, the microbrewery located in Ham-Nord, in the regional county municipality of Arthabaska, is part of the Centre-du-Québec tourism region.

TRANSPORTATION

There is no public transit system servicing Ham-Sud and Ham-Nord. To get there, you'll have to manage on your own. Parking at the regional park is free.

TRAIL INFORMATION

Parc régional du Mont-Ham
819 828-3608
montham.ca

TOURIST INFORMATION

Bureau d'information touristique de la MRC des Sources
39 rue du Dépôt
Danville, QC
J0A 1A0
819 839-2911
tourismedessources.com

Tourisme Cantons-de-l'Est
easterntownships.org

Tourisme Centre-du-Québec
tourismecentreduquebec.com

LA GRANGE PARDUE

It's on his family farm spanning three generations that Stéphane Turcotte got the idea to open a work cooperative and a microbrewery, La Grange Pardue (The Lost Barn; the word *pardue* reflects the local way to pronounce *perdue*, meaning "lost"). With his pals, Philippe Langlois and Stéphane Martin, Stéphane Turcotte has helped build a strong local community based on a project that pays homage to the region and its fruit. La Grange Pardue is the first brewery farm in the Centre-du-Québec region. Educational panels have been set up to help visitors learn about the crops, brewing techniques, and products as they stroll around the farm. You can book several different beer-related activities and guided tours. At the tasting room, you'll be seduced by the selection of different beers, with names that echo the local dialect. If you happen to be seated by the bay window as you sip on your beer, you can watch the making of the beer right before your own eyes. La Grange Pardue is an experience that will satisfy both your thirst and your curiosity!

BREWERY

La Grange Pardue
261 QC-216
Ham-Nord, QC
G0P 1A0
819 344-2200
lagrangepardue.com

NEARBY BREWERY

Microbrasserie Moulin 7
294 boulevard Saint-Luc
Val-des-Sources, QC
J1T 2W2
819 716-0686
moulin7.com

WHERE TO TRY THIS BEER

Right on-site.

WHERE TO BUY THIS BEER

Right on-site.

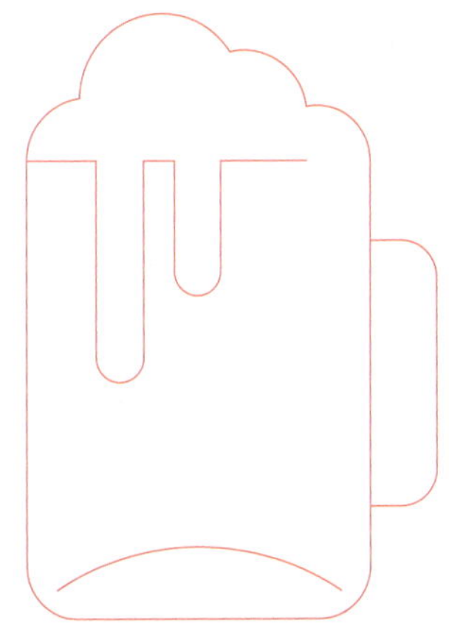

CHARLEVOIX

BAIE-SAINT-PAUL

A HIKE DRIPPING WITH CHARLEVOIX CHARM

STARTING POINT	DESTINATION
PARC DU GOUFFRE	LE SAINT-PUB, MICROBRASSERIE CHARLEVOIX
BEER	**DIFFICULTY**
FLACATOUNE	MODERATE
DOG FRIENDLY	**SEASON**
YES, ON LEASH	YEAR-ROUND
FEES	**DURATION**
NO	5 HOURS
MAP REFERENCE	**LENGTH**
AVAILABLE ONLINE	14.6 (OR 18) KM
HIGHLIGHTS	**ELEVATION CHANGE**
PARC DU GOUFFRE, BAIE-SAINT-PAUL, CULTURAL GEM, RIVIÈRE DU GOUFFRE	ASCENT: 251 M DESCENT: 252 M

FILTERED STRONG PALE ALE

GOLDEN, CLEAR

FRUIT, HOPS, SPICES

MALTY, SPICES, CITRUS

BITTERNESS

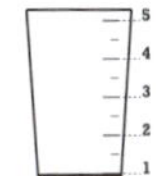

SWEETNESS

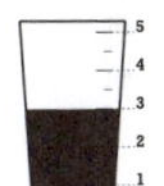

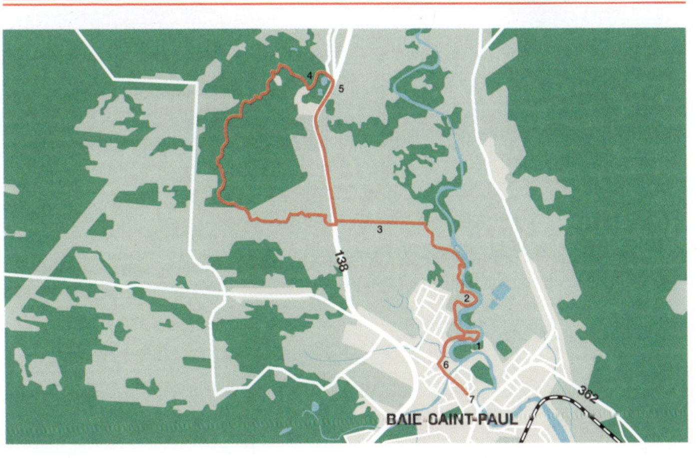

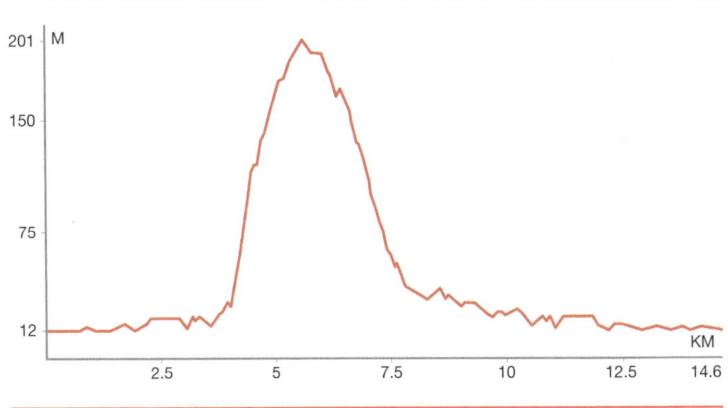

HIKE DESCRIPTION

Immerse yourself in the scenery, culture, and charm of Baie-Saint-Paul in the picturesque region of Charlevoix. Then make it even better with a Flacatoune beer.

Baie-Saint-Paul will charm the pants off you, with its built heritage, small-town feel, and numerous boutiques that sell crafts and other local products. But first, check out its larger-than-life surroundings.

Sentier du Gouffre, a trail that is part of Quebec's Sentier national (National Trail) and connects two other trails (Robert-Leblanc and Les Florent), starts at Parc du Gouffre in the heart of the village. From the park, the trail cuts through a variety of settings, from marshes and land occasionally flooded by beavers to evergreen forests and agricultural fields. There are also pretty views over the valley, of the neighboring mountains, and around Baie-Saint-Paul.

Your journey starts at Parc du Gouffre[1] on rue Saint-Édouard. The way to the trailhead, 1.7 kilometers away, is clearly marked. In fact, the entire hike is well marked and easy to follow in both directions. You'll find the trail is shared with another trail, Sentier Robert-Leblanc, which is multipurpose and used for many different activities.

First, follow the river Rivière du Gouffre[2] across a striking carpet of ferns that spread out into a wooded area between the marsh and the beaver dams. Take the trails shooting off toward the river to see the beavers' work for yourself.

When you reach the official start point to the hike, there'll be a sign advising you to stick to the trail in order to respect the environment and avoid encroaching on private property. The first section rises slowly and then runs, for a few meters, adjacent to a large, open area before plunging you back into the woods, which leads to a dirt road. Take the road to the left, where you'll cross some large, organic farm fields[3], and get your first good glimpse of the mountains in the distance.

At the end, follow the arrows along the roadside that lead over a small, wooden footbridge and through tall grass. After a few meters, you'll have to cross Route 138. Be careful, as heavy-weight vehicles use this road at high speeds.

From the other side of the road, you might feel as though you're trespassing, and that's because there's a private property to go around on your left. After this, there's another dirt road running alongside a pasture, usually with a few cows casually grazing. You're getting pretty high-up at this point, so turn around and take in the gorgeous view of Baie-Saint-Paul and the surrounding area.

At the top, at the back of the field, go into the woods. Your calf muscles are in for a good workout as you zigzag through the trees. The trail isn't always easy to follow, but the red arrows are.

After a good climb, you'll arrive at a picnic area, where you'll climb even further. As you walk along a clearing, you will find yourself on the perimeter of another field. From this point on, there may be muddy sections and you'll definitely have to walk through tall grass.

Now, it's time for another change of scenery as you head back into the brush and go farther and farther away from civilization. Notice the peace and tranquility all around. Make your way through this new environment. Eventually, you'll come to a small passageway made of large stones leading out of the woods.

Next, there's a small muddy ditch to cross. You may find the change in scenery a little disappointing, but keep your eyes on the prize and just get through this bumpy, deforested section (minding your step, of course). You'll soon be rewarded with another forest on the other side, and from there keep going until you get to Le Genévrier[4], a campground and the endpoint for Sentier du Gouffre.

From here, you have two options (This hike can be done in the winter using snowshoes, in which case avoid option number 2, Route 138 shortcut, for your own safety.):

1. The first option[5] involves retracing your steps and getting a chance to see the various landscapes under a new light. It is prettier and a bit more adventurous than option two.

2. The second option is faster but requires you to walk for about 20 minutes along a busy road. Start by crossing the campground until you get to the main entrance near Route 138. Turn right. Walk against the traffic and **remain alert at all times**. The second option avoids the steeper sections of option one and shortens your walk by about an hour. Keep going until you arrive at the place where you crossed the road earlier. Then, get back on the trail until you reach Parc du Gouffre.

Whatever option you choose, you will end up in the same place the adventure began: Parc du Gouffre. From there, follow the signs for Sentier de la Baie (or go left on Saint-Édouard and left again on Saint-Jean-Baptiste) to return to the heart of the village.

Take some time to stroll around Saint-Jean-Baptiste[6] and let its artistic and cultural feel soak in. This is also a good time to check out some of those boutiques and craft shops and load up on local products. Don't forget to admire the pretty houses either—charming icons of the downtown core. You can even go down to the river—just turn around when you're finished to make your way back.

This hike's brewery, Le Saint-Pub, Microbrasserie Charlevoix[7], is on your right (or on your left if you walked down to the river!). Settle in on the patio and sip on a refreshing Flacatoune, an experience made all the better by Baie-Saint-Paul's easy-going atmosphere and beauty!

Other options:
The Charlevoix region is a true paradise for hikers who love peaks and aren't afraid of a vigorous climb. Sentier du Gouffre was chosen to shake things up and because it connects directly to Baie-Saint-Paul's downtown core. If a greater challenge interests you, take Route 381 toward Saint-Urbain and make your way to Sentier du Mont du Dôme in the Zec des Martres (a *zec* is a French acronym for "controlled harvest zone"), for a 7.8 km, moderate-level loop located about 30 kilometers from Baie-Saint-Paul.

You could also follow Route 138 toward Quebec City and turn right onto rue Principale, direction Petite-Rivière-Saint-François. That's where you'll find Sentier du Mont à Liguori (part of the long-distance trail Sentier des Caps de Charlevoix), a strenuous, 15.4 km trail that has gorgeous views of the river.

TRANSPORTATION

From the bus station or train station, make your way on foot to Ambroise-Fafard. Take a right and go as far as rue Sainte-Anne (called Saint-Jean-Baptiste on the left). Turn left and then right onto Saint-Édouard, which puts you at Parc du Gouffre. If you are driving, leave your car at the park.

TRAIL INFORMATION

Tourisme Charlevoix (see below)

TOURIST INFORMATION

Tourisme Charlevoix
6 rue Saint-Jean-Baptiste
Baie-Saint-Paul, QC
G3Z 1L7
418 665-4454
tourisme-charlevoix.com

MICROBRASSERIE CHARLEVOIX

Frédérick Tremblay and Caroline Bandulet (romantic partners and business associates) shared a passion for beer making, which led to the establishment of Microbrasserie Charlevoix in 1998. A few years after, Nicolas Marrant joined the team, bringing with him considerable brewing experience. Microbrasserie Charlevoix has been busy making beers in the heart of Baie-Saint-Paul ever since, including some Belgian-inspired beers. Despite a considerable expansion in 2008, the team has held on to its craft beer roots and continues to produce quality beer.

BREWERY

Microbrasserie Charlevoix
6 rue Paul-René Tremblay
Baie-Saint-Paul, QC
G3Z 3E4
microbrasserie.com

WHERE TO TRY THIS BEER

Saint-Pub, Microbrasserie Charlevoix
2 rue Racine
Baie-Saint-Paul, QC
G3Z 2P8
saint-pub.com

WHERE TO BUY THIS BEER

At the shop annexed to the brewery (rue Paul-René Tremblay) and in most grocery stores, corner stores, and specialty shops in the region.

CHAUDIÈRE-APPALACHES

BUCKLAND AND SAINT-PHILÉMON

CONQUERING THE CRÊTE DES GRIVES LOOP

STARTING POINT	DESTINATION
RECEPTION AREA, MASSIF DU SUD REGIONAL PARK	RECEPTION AREA, MASSIF DU SUD REGIONAL PARK
BEER	**DIFFICULTY**
KÖLSCH DE BELLECHASSE	MODERATE
DOG FRIENDLY	**SEASON**
YES, ON LEASH	YEAR-ROUND
FEES	**DURATION**
YES, PAY AT RECEPTION	4 HOURS
MAP REFERENCE	**LENGTH**
AVAILABLE AT PARK RECEPTION	11 KM
HIGHLIGHTS	**ELEVATION CHANGE**
CRÊTE DES GRIVES SUMMIT, VILLAGE OF BUCKLAND, OLD-GROWTH FOREST	ASCENT: 488 M DESCENT: 489 M

GERMAN EXTRA PALE ALE

GOLDEN, LIGHT

HINTS OF GRASS, GRAIN

GRAIN, GRASSY

BITTERNESS

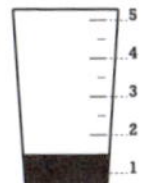

SWEETNESS

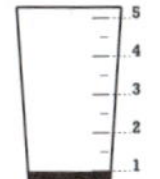

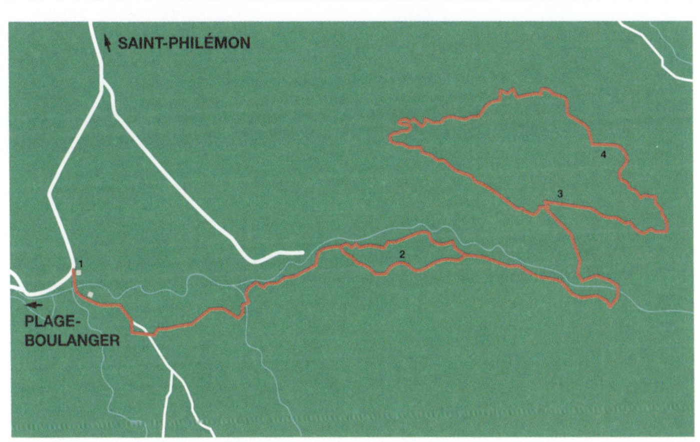

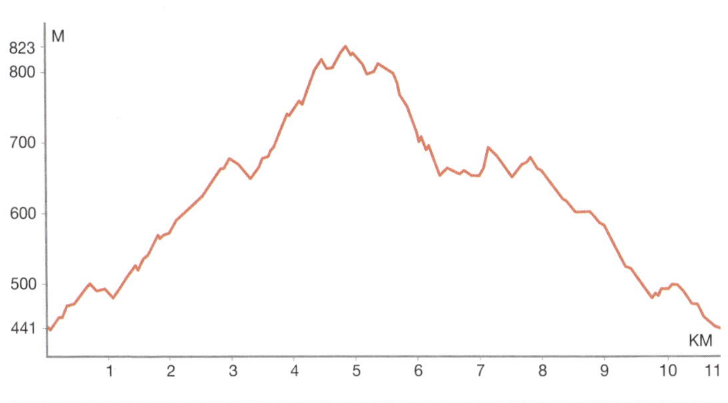

HIKE DESCRIPTION

Hike the mountains of the Massif du Sud regional park and find yourself in the middle of an ancient forest. There's a hefty climb that is sure to make you thirst for that beer at the end!

With an area of 103 km^2, the Parc du Massif du Sud is a regional park located in Bellechasse and is part of the Appalachian Mountains. The park is popular with winter-sport enthusiasts, but hikers also flock there year-round to take advantage of its 71 km trail network. The park borders the villages of Saint-Philémon, where you'll find the reception office, and Notre-Dame-Auxiliatrice-de-Buckland, where you'll find the microbrewery Microbrasserie de Bellechasse in the heart of the village.

Leave your car near the park's reception area[1]. Sign in and pay an admission fee. Take a moment to hit up the toilets and fill your water bottle. In the fall, during hunting season, some areas of the park are closed, while others are shared spaces for a few weeks. Inquire at the park reception for more information on trail access and the necessary precautions.

The Crête des Grives trail starts to the right of the reception building. Take the gravel road, cross the wooden bridge, and then keep going until you come to a fork with signs for different hikes. Turn left and go under the little wooden archway. From there, just follow the blue signs. Whenever there's a choice of directions to take, there'll be a sign to show you the way and a map showing you your location.

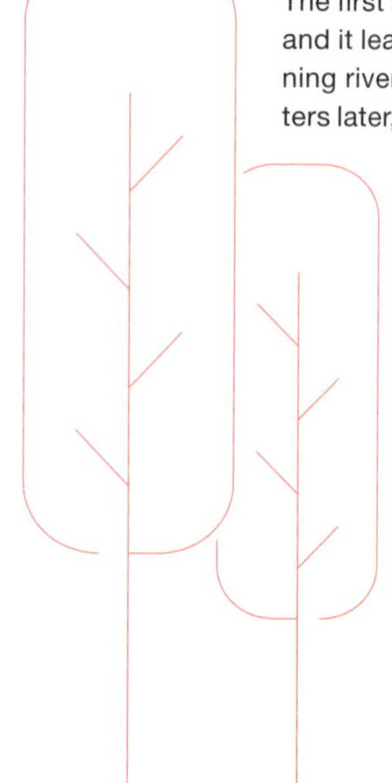

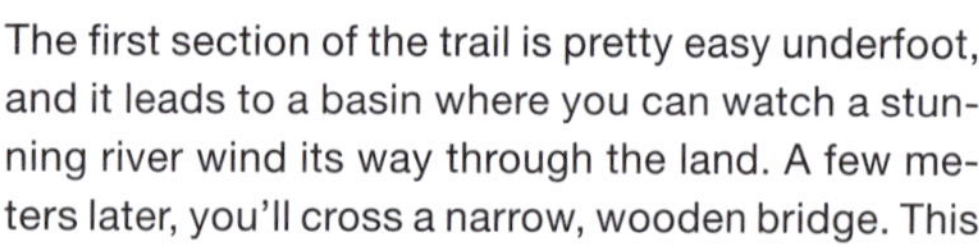

The first section of the trail is pretty easy underfoot, and it leads to a basin where you can watch a stunning river wind its way through the land. A few meters later, you'll cross a narrow, wooden bridge. This is where you enter the 51-hectare, old-growth forest of Ruisseau-Beaudoin[2], where yellow birch and balsam fir dominate the landscape.

An old-growth forest is one that has reached its peak, its ultimate state of stability, where plant and animal species co-exist in perfect equilibrium. The telltale feature of such forests is the presence of very old trees, and it can take several hundred years for a forest to reach this stage.

About a third of the way into your hike, the terrain becomes more uneven and the climbs get steeper and steeper. At the first fork, go left, while at the second fork, go right[3]. You are now just 1.1 kilometers from the summit, so hang in there!

When you're at the top, you'll see a sign guiding you toward a vantage point 20 meters to your right, but keep going. Shortly thereafter, on the left, you'll reach another viewpoint[4]. This one is in the heart of the hilly region of Chaudière-Appalaches, 825 meters above sea level. The view at the top is said to be one of the best in the whole park.

Had enough? Keep going to the right. Start your 2.4 km descent until you reach the last fork, and then retrace your steps to the first one. This time, take the trail on the left for a change of scenery. This will take you back to the narrow bridge where you'll happen upon, once again, that beautiful river. To get back to the reception, just keep following the signs through the woods.

You're back at your starting point, and your legs are tired by now—plus you're thirsty. So, quickly hop in the car and take Route du Massif-du-Sud to the end, and then turn left and make your way to Notre-Dame-Auxiliatrice-de-Buckland. Locate the church (on your left) in the heart of the village. Why? Because right next to it is your final destination: Pub de la Contrée—Microbrasserie de Bellechasse.

Find an indoor seat, for no other reason than the locally crafted décor and rustic atmosphere, and order the Kölsch de Bellechasse, a German-inspired brew made from 100% Quebec hops. The pub serves up stupendously delicious meals featuring local ingredients, so consider grabbing a bite as well.

TRANSPORTATION

No public transit system services the area. It's best to find your own way to the regional park and the microbrewery.

TRAIL INFORMATION

Parc régional du Massif du Sud (reception)
300 route du Massif
Saint-Philémon, QC
G0R 4A0
418 469-2228
massifdusud.com

TOURIST INFORMATION

Tourisme Bellechasse
418 884-3726
bellechasse.chaudiereappalaches.com

Tourisme Chaudière-Appalaches
418 831-4411
chaudiereappalaches.com

PUB DE LA CONTRÉE – MICROBRASSERIE DE BELLECHASSE

In 2012, craft beer brewmaster Gabriel Paquet and Anabelle Goupil (CEO and general manager, respectively) decided to create a gathering place in the heart of the village, which at the time had been experiencing a population decline. That's how the brewing cooperative came to be built in a converted credit union at the foot of the Appalachian Mountain of Massif du Sud. Gabriel and Anabelle are clearly committed to showcasing regional products: the hops come from the Beauce region, the malt from Lotbinière, and other ingredients from Bellechasse. Their regional pride even shines through in the names of the beers, each of which is named after a local community.

BREWERY

Microbrasserie de Bellechasse
2020 rue de l'Église
Buckland, QC
G0R 1G0
418 789-4444
microbrasseriedebellechasse.ca

WHERE TO TRY THIS BEER

On-site

WHERE TO BUY THIS BEER

Épicerie-Boulangerie de Buckland (located across the street)
4285 Route Principale
Buckland, QC
G0R 1G0

CÔTE-NORD

TADOUSSAC

A TALE OF FJORDS AND WHALES

STARTING POINT	DESTINATION
FISH CULTURE STATION	MICROBRASSERIE DE TADOUSSAC
BEER	**DIFFICULTY**
BUSE	MODERATE
DOG FRIENDLY	**SEASON**
YES, ON LEASH, VILLAGE TRAILS ONLY	MID-MAY TO MID-OCTOBER
FEES	**DURATION**
YES, SÉPAQ RATES APPLY	5 HOURS
MAP REFERENCE	**LENGTH**
AVAILABLE AT THE TADOUSSAC TOURIST INFORMATION OFFICE	11 KM
HIGHLIGHTS	**ELEVATION CHANGE**
SAGUENAY FJORD, L'ANSE À L'EAU LAKE, VILLAGE OF TADOUSSAC, ST. LAWRENCE ESTUARY	ASCENT: 455 M DESCENT: 457 M

COPPER ALE

COPPERY

RYE, BISCUITS

APRICOTS, DRIED FRUIT

BITTERNESS

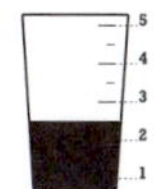

SWEETNESS

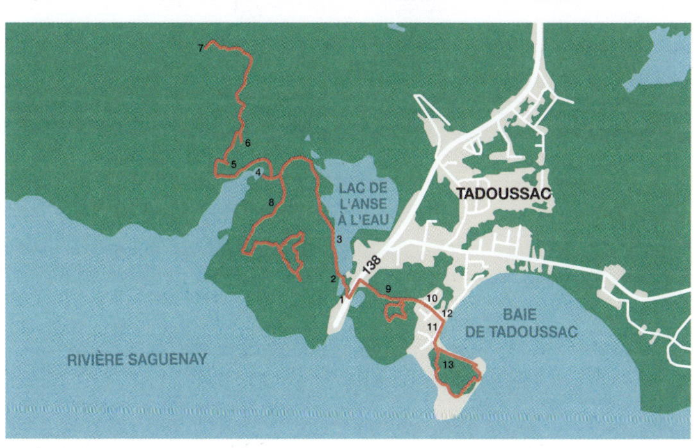

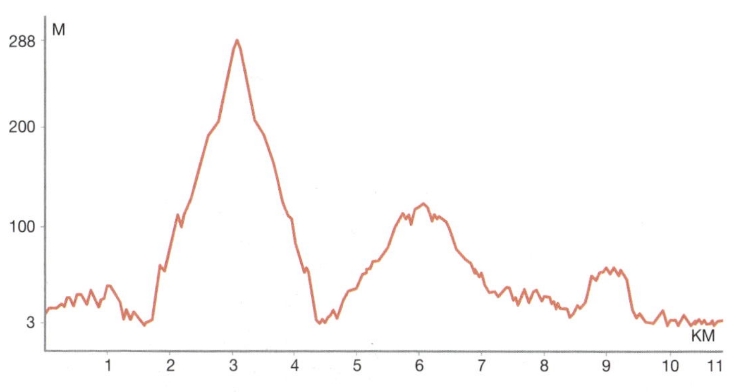

HIKE DESCRIPTION

Survey a section of a fjord-side trail, maybe encounter a whale, amble along a beach, and wash ashore at a local brewery: the Microbrasserie Tadoussac.

In Saguenay Fjord National Park (a provincial park of Quebec), the 40-odd kilometers of Sentier du Fjord connects the villages of Baie Sainte-Marguerite, in Saguenay, to Tadoussac, the gateway to Manicouagan on the North Shore.

Today, you'll explore one section of the trail in the vicinity of Baie de Tadoussac. Starting in the village, this hike will take you from mountain to hill, and you can keep the adventure going with two other short trails: Sentier de la Colline-de-L'Anse-à-l'Eau and Sentier de la Pointe de l'Islet.

On Route 138 (rue du Bateau-Passeur), close to where the ferry docks, take the alleyway to the left below the fish hatchery[1]. The route is fairly obvious: just head for the other side of the dam where the trail actually starts. Here is where you will have to pay your SÉPAQ fee, at the self-payment station[2]. Then, you'll start on a pleasant lakeside walk along Lac de l'Anse à l'Eau[3].

The trail is generally well marked. First, follow the signs toward Mont Adéla-Lessard. You'll find that sometimes the path rises gently, and other times, it climbs sharply. The trail offers one view after another, so the payoff is immediate.

Next, you'll come upon Belvédère de l'Anse à la Barque[4] and two other lookouts[5,6], all of which offer views of striking landscapes. Once you're at the peak[7], take a deep breath. You have arrived, and it was just a 3 km walk! Take a moment to marvel and then retrace your steps, because the adventure isn't over yet!

When you're back down, on your right you'll find a trail leading to the hill at L'Anse-à-la-Barque[8], a loop that's a little more than one kilometer and has other lookout points, each one more breathtaking than the last. A good portion of this trail is over a rocky promontory. If you just follow the peach-colored circles directly on the rocks, you'll find your way. Finish the loop and then take Sentier du Fjord again on your right, to find the way back to the starting point.

From the starting point, cross the road and take a slight left. Pass the parking lot across from the fish farm and get on Sentier de la Colline-de-l'Anse-à-l'Eau[9]. This is an easy, 1.1-km loop formerly known as La Coupe Trail (the hardest parts of the hike are behind you!).

You will quickly find yourself at the crest of the hill, surrounded by trees, smack-dab in the middle of a 360° view that includes part of the Saguenay fjord, the village, Tadoussac beach, and the St. Lawrence estuary. This trail terminates at the end of rue de la Coupe-de-l'Islet[10].

Walk down the street until you get to rue du Bord-de-l'Eau[11]. At the corner, your microbrewery, Microbrasserie de Tadoussac[12], is on your right. You've put in a good effort. If you decide to end your adventure now, no one can blame you. But you still have the option, because it's so worth it, to squeeze just a bit more juice from the lemon.

On board? Terrific! Take a right onto rue du Bord-de-l'Eau and climb the stairs located at the bend. You're now on Sentier de la Pointe-de-l'Islet[13], a 900-meter loop that, as promised, offers a few new views of the surrounding landscape, including a marine mammal observation point. With a stroke of good luck, you just might see a whale or two.
Complete the loop and take rue du Bord-de-l'Eau back. Now it's time to head to the microbrewery where the recommended beer is a Buse to accompany a nice, warm meal.

TRANSPORTATION

You can get to Tadoussac by train or bus. From the station, go down rue du Bateau-Passeur for about 300 meters. The trailhead is on your right.

If you got to Tadoussac on your own, there is a SÉPAQ parking lot across from the hatchery. From there, just cross rue du Bateau-Passeur to find the trailhead, about 100 meters beyond on your left. It's not too far from where you arrived.

TRAIL INFORMATION

Parc national du Fjord du Saguenay (for Sentier du Fjord)
418 272-1556
sepaq.com/pq/sag

Office de tourisme de Tadoussac (for Sentier de la Colline-de-l'Anse-à-l'Eau and Sentier de la Pointe de l'Islet) see below

TOURIST INFORMATION

Maison du tourisme de Tadoussac
197 rue des Pionniers
Tadoussac, QC
G0T 2A0
418 235-4744
tadoussac.com

Tourisme Côte-Nord
tourismecote-nord.com

MICROBRASSERIE TADOUSSAC

In 2017, Martin Fournier and Shawn Thompson opened Microbrasserie Tadoussac. Here Sylvain Langlois, aided by Éric Dufour, is in charge of the brewing. The beers are set apart thanks to the flavors of the coast and the artistic flair and penchant for experimentation of the brewers. Every beer at this microbrewery is a reflection of the region, its wildlife, geography, and culture. The brewery boasts an exceptional location matched only by the ambiance, food menu, and beer. Proceeds from the sale of some beers go to not-for-profit organizations.

BREWERY

Microbrasserie Tadoussac
145 rue du Bord de l'Eau
Tadoussac, QC
G0T 2A0
418 980-4900
microtadoussac.com

WHERE TO TRY THIS BEER

On-site, in the tasting room.

WHERE TO BUY THIS BEER

At the shop connected to the microbrewery and in several shops throughout the province.

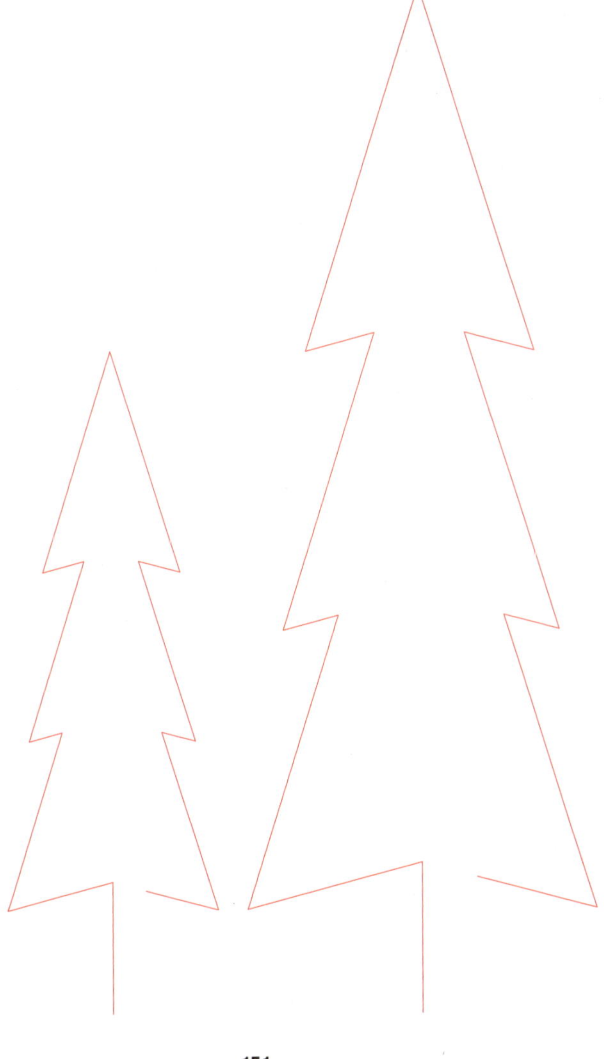

GASPÉ PENINSULA

CARLETON-SUR-MER

A HEARTY HIKE IN THE HEART OF CHALEUR BAY

STARTING POINT	DESTINATION
CAP FERRÉ PARKING LOT	CAP FERRÉ PARKING LOT
BEER	**DIFFICULTY**
ST-BARNABÉ	MODERATE TO STRENUOUS
DOG FRIENDLY	**SEASON**
NO	END OF JUNE TO EARLY OCTOBER
FEES	**DURATION**
FREE ON WALKING TRAILS, FEE TO ACCESS THE SUMMIT	4 HOURS
MAP REFERENCE	**LENGTH**
AVAILABLE AT THE CARLETON-SUR-MER VISITOR CENTER	10.2 KM
HIGHLIGHTS	**ELEVATION CHANGE**
MONT SAINT-JOSEPH, VILLAGE OF CARLETON-SUR-MER, WATERFALLS	ASCENT: 563 M DESCENT: 564 M

DRY STOUT

BLACK, HAZY

ROASTED COFFEE, CHERRIES

COFFEE, CHOCOLATE

BITTERNESS · SWEETNESS

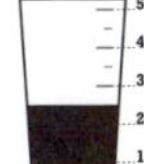

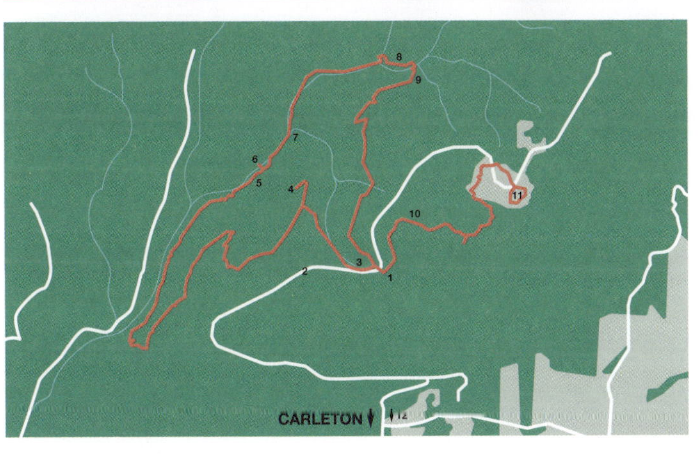

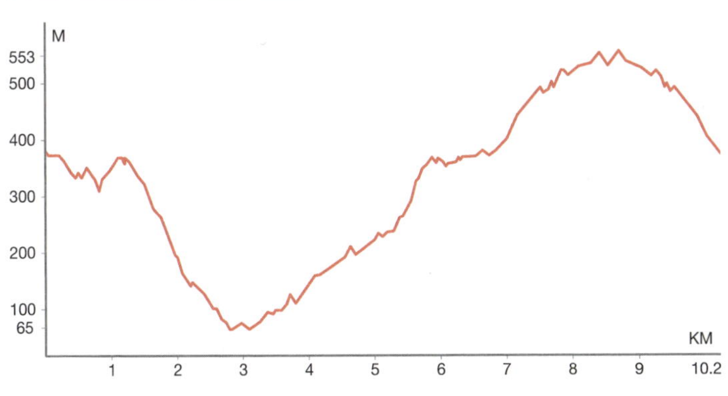

HIKE DESCRIPTION

Climb to the top of Mont Saint-Joseph, cross waterfalls, climb, and climb some more until finally returning back down to the village for a nice Naufrageur beer.

Mont Saint-Joseph, a 555-meter peak located only 5 kilometers from the coast, is perfectly situated in the heart of Chaleur Bay. The region Carleton-sur-Mer is a hiker's paradise. There are 30 kilometers of trails that take you up to the top of Mont Saint-Joseph and Mount Carleton and down to the valleys, along flowing rivers and cascading falls.

The trail for today's hike, La Grande Virée, starts in the Cap Ferré parking lot (P2)[1], which you can reach via rue de la Montagne[2].

Follow the signs for Sentier Le Taguine[3]. After a few meters, you'll arrive at a fork with three options. Head toward the middle, which is a pedestrian-only pathway. Here begins a long descent (gentle at first before becoming increasingly physical) along a trail that is fairly wide, well maintained, and especially easy to follow. You won't have to check to see if you are on the right path, so stop worrying and simply enjoy your time in the woods, as you make your way down toward the river.

One exception is that, on the left-hand side, you can walk to a lookout[4] located about 200 meters beyond the intersection. Go out to enjoy the view and then come back and keep going on Le Taguine.

After a while, you'll arrive at a waterfall. Cross the small, wooden bridge[5] (why not take a second to splash a bit of water on your face?) and then take the stairs. Head for the lookout[6] on your left (barely 20 meters separates you from a magnificent view), then come back and cross the river again and get ready for the next climb. On your left, there's yet another lookout (go for it, it's worth it), and to your right, the trail continues its ascent.

Not long after this, at the fork, take Sentier des Éperlan[7] toward the river. You'll walk along the water's edge for a bit before the trail starts to narrow, wind, and zigzag upward.

At the next intersection, there'll be a trail going straight ahead. Don't take it (there's a sign saying it's a one-way bike trail). Take Sentier des Rescapés[8] and continue your climb. This section of the trail is shared with cyclists, so be careful and yield as necessary.

A little further on and you will come across another fork in the trail. Take Sentier Le Monti[9] on your right (hikers only), which quickly leads to a bridge spanning a river (this is a good location for a snack). Your climb isn't over quite yet, so take advantage of this spot to recharge your batteries!

Ever so gently, Le Monti will lead you back to the parking lot. Here, you could say "I've had enough" and hop back into your car, heading straight for the brewery (no one would be the wiser!).

But since you've come this far, why not take Sentier Cap Ferré[10] and hike the 1.8 km distance to the top of Mont Saint-Joseph[11], an elevation of 555 meters. You might tell yourself you've had enough climbing and seen enough panoramas for one day, but the next one is not like the others. What awaits is a spectacular view of the small, lively town of Carleton-sur-Mer, the tourist hub of Chaleur Bay, with a backdrop of the sea and the mountains. On a clear day, you can even make out the neighboring province of New Brunswick. There is a fee to access the summit.

After you've composed yourself (the view is truly moving!), retrace your steps back to your car. Take rue de la Montagne as far as boulevard Perron (Route 132), and then turn left. The famous microbrewery Le Naufrageur[12] is located 130 meters from there. Fall in love with the relaxed atmosphere and order yourself a St-Barnabé, the finest of dry stouts.

Notes:
Daredevils may wish to walk or bike from the village via rue de la Montagne. Doing so adds 12.6 kilometers to the hike (6.3 kilometers out and back). The steep road snakes its way to the summit, but you have to be careful as the road is shared by cars, cyclists, and brave pedestrians.

Other options:
You could also do the hike in the other direction, for example, by starting with Mont Saint-Joseph and ending as expected, or you could start at Le Monti and finish with Le Taguine. In my view, the most logical choice is the one described here, but there is no wrong decision. Either way, the beer won't hold it against you.

TRANSPORTATION

The Carleton station is centrally located in the village. If you are arriving by your own means, the easiest solution is to park at the Cap Ferré parking lot, do the hike, and then drive to the microbrewery.

TRAIL INFORMATION

Mont Saint-Joseph
418 364-2276, extension 1
montsaintjoseph.com

TOURIST INFORMATION

Bureau d'accueil touristique de Carleton-sur-Mer
774 boulevard Perron
Carleton-sur-Mer, QC
G0C 1J0
418 364-3544
carletonsurmer.com

Tourisme Gaspésie
tourisme-gaspesie.com

LE NAUFRAGEUR

The story behind Le Naufrageur (The Shipwrecker) is one of a shared vision, dreams come true, and pirate progeny (yes, you read that correctly!). Sébastien and Louis-Franck Valade were initiated into the world of brewing early on by a father who loved to brew. The brothers dreamed of opening a microbrewery, but first their mother wanted a bakery. La Mie Véritable, a café and bakery, opened in 1997. Le Naufrageur finally opened its doors in 2008, after Christelle and Philippe came along and helped add a chapter to this adorable family tale. Today, the microbrewery has more than 30 beers on tap (four of which are always on offer). Most of the beers are named after a ship that sank either off the Gaspé Peninsula or in the lower St. Lawrence (Bas-Saint-Laurent), thus merging a family story with the history of a region.

BREWERY

Le Naufrageur
586 boulevard Perron
Carleton, QC
G0C 1J0
418 364-5440
lenaufrageur.com

Open daily during the summer period, with reduced hours from early November to early May.

WHERE TO TRY THIS BEER

Right on-site.

WHERE TO BUY THIS BEER

At the micro market annexed to the brewery (during the summer period) or at La Mie Véritable bakery located next to the microbrewery.

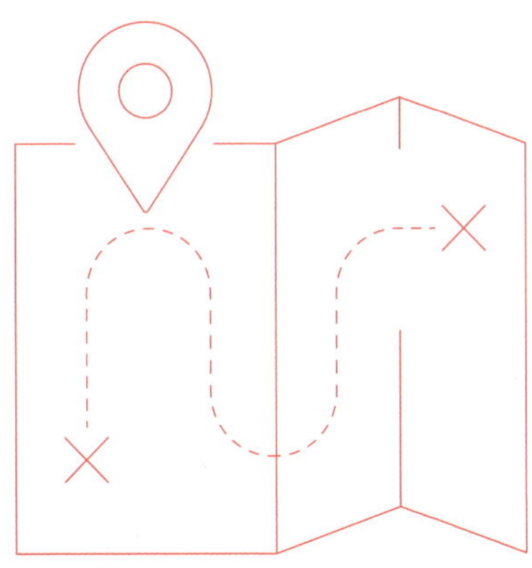

PERCÉ

AN ENCHANTED FOREST AND BREATHTAKING VIEWS

STARTING POINT	DESTINATION
GEOPARK VISITOR CENTER	PUB LE PIT CARIBOU
BEER	DIFFICULTY
BLONDE DE L'ANSE	MODERATE
DOG FRIENDLY	SEASON
YES, ON LEASH	YEAR-ROUND
FEES	DURATION
NO (BUT THERE IS A FEE TO ACCESS THE SUSPENDED PLATFORM)	4.75 HOURS
MAP REFERENCE	LENGTH
AVAILABLE AT THE GEOPARK RECEPTION AND THROUGHOUT THE TRAILS	14 KM
HIGHLIGHTS	ELEVATION CHANGE
VIEW OF PERCÉ ROCK NATURAL ARCH, BONAVENTURE ISLAND AND THE SEA; MONT SAINTE-ANNE (TABLE À ROLAND); CAVE; CREVASSE; MAGIC FOREST	ASCENT: 588 M DESCENT: 588 M

GOLDEN ALE

GOLDEN, LIGHT

GRAINS, FLORAL HINTS

GRAINS, FRUITY, REFRESHING

BITTERNESS SWEETNESS

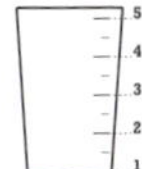

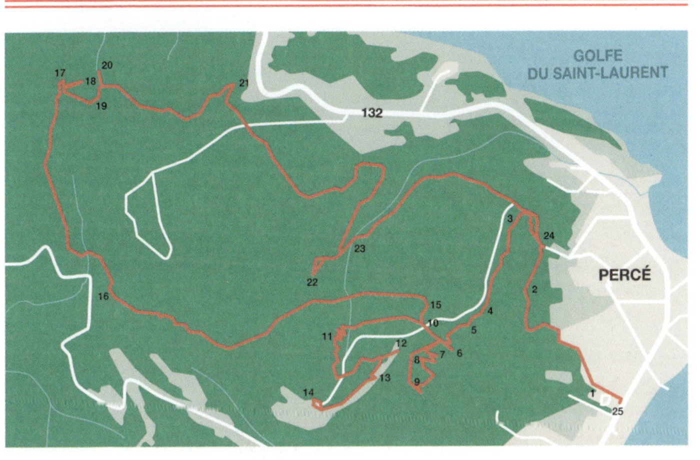

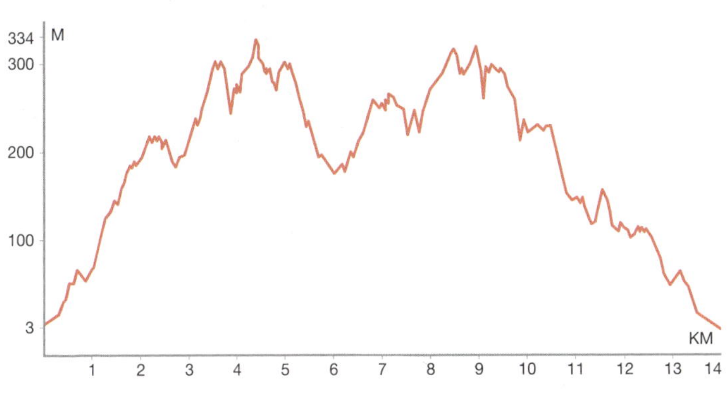

HIKE DESCRIPTION

Cliffs, caves, the sea, a crevasse, a magical forest, and an exceptional view of Percé Rock and Bonaventure Island...what more could you ask for? What about a refreshing, frothy ale from Pit Caribou?

UNESCO geoparks are geographic spaces that are managed according to a global concept of nature preservation, sustainable development, and education. The Percé UNESCO Global Geopark contains 500 million years of history, evidence of bygone geological eras, and breathtaking scenery!

The hike starts behind the visitor center[1], and the path to the trailhead is well marked. First, cross the geopark's campground and then take Sentier des Arpenteurs[2] for 600 meters. This is a gentle elevation—a nice way to start—that has, along the way, interpretation panels about Percé and its legendary characters!

At the intersection, take Sentier des Belvédères[3], which is still fairly easy and leads to two lookouts[4,5] where you get your first high-angle views of Percé and its famous rock. The trail is very well marked and heavily trafficked, so you'll have no trouble finding your way. After 1.1 kilometers, you'll reach a suspended glass platform[6]. If you're brave enough, for a fee, you can test your fear of heights. Otherwise, keep going, because there'll be other opportunities to get an incredible view.

Right after the platform, take the trail leading to the magical forest[7]. This is a 900-meter loop where the curved tree trunks—possibly caused by the earth giving way a long time ago—make the landscape seem almost surreal. Belvédère de la Grive[8] and Belvédère du Nid du Corbeau[9] are two lookouts with views of the "bottomless hole" that will leave you befuddled.

Back at the start of the loop, near the platform, take a left. You will pass by toilets and cross Chemin du Mont-Sainte-Anne[10]. From there, get back on Sentier des Belvédères, where the trail now becomes slightly more difficult. Zigzag your way up to the top of Mont Sainte-Anne.

You will pass by three lookouts[11,12,13], two of which offer a preview of the view from the summit. Look down and you'll see Bonaventure Island (the largest migratory bird sanctuary in North America), Percé Rock, the city of Percé, and water as far as the eye can see. At the top is Table à Roland (Roland's Table), the geopark's high point where geological history and ancient symbolism come together. You'll find a small chapel and place of meditation[14]. Absorb the splendor of the moment and then head back the way you came.

At the intersection of Chemin du Mont-Sainte-Anne and Sentier des Belvédères, veer off on Sentier des Sources to your left[15]. Take this trail for 1.7 kilometers until the next fork. Then, on your right, take Sentier Les Pieds Croches[16], which takes you to the Crevasse, an enormous crack in the rock that is 60 meters deep and the result of some geomorphological event that happened here long ago.

Follow Sentier de la Crevasse toward two viewpoints[17,18] located on this giant crack, and then make a U-turn to get on Sentier de la Grande Coupe[19]. Shortly after, pop out to the viewpoint[20] on your left and then keep going for a little more than 2 kilometers. Go past another lookout, Belvédère du Pic[21], and then head to the cave[22] where you'll be greeted by a waterfall and an otherworldliness.

From this point, follow Chemin de la Grotte[23] (a road for cars, so please be vigilant), which later becomes rue de l'Église[24] and then leads to Sentier des Arpenteurs and back to your starting point.

Cross the campground, go around the reception, and then keep going straight until you hit Route 132. Turn right where the patio of pub Pit Caribou has been waiting for you[25]. The beers on offer are brewed not far from here, at the Pit Caribou microbrewery. So how about a nice pale ale to cap off the day?

TRANSPORTATION

Percé is reachable by coach, and the station is located along Route 132, not very far from the geopark and microbrewery. You'll have to walk about 400 meters south to get to the geopark.

If you are coming by car, you can park (for a fee) at the Percé Geopark reception.

TRAIL INFORMATION

Percé UNESCO Global Geopark
180 Route 132 Ouest
Percé, QC
G0C 2L0
418 782-5112
geoparcdeperce.com

TOURIST INFORMATION

Bureau d'accueil touristique de Percé
142 Route 132 Ouest
Percé, QC
G0C 2L0
418 782-5448
perce.info

Tourisme Gaspésie
www.tourisme-gaspesie.com

PIT CARIBOU

In 2007, brewers Francis Joncas and Benoît Couillard teamed up with Brad Murray to open the first microbrewery in eastern, mainland Quebec, in L'Anse-à-Beaufils. In 2012, the old general store in the heart of Percé was converted into a tasting room to make room for more beer lovers without sacrificing any of the place's character. Since they began, things have really taken off and the Pit Caribou has only gained in popularity. Two years after opening, Benoît founded Brasserie Auval in Val-d'Espoir, while Francis and Brad are seeing success with another project: Brett et Sauvage, a nanobrewery (an even smaller microbrewery) not far from Percé. In 2019, Pit Caribou was sold to Vincent Coderre and Jean-François Neliss. The tradition of making quality Gaspé beer has been handed over to brewmaster Pascal Thériault.

BREWERY

Pit Caribou
27 rue de l'Anse
L'Anse-à-Beaufils, QC
G0C 1G0
pitcaribou.com

NEARBY BREWERIES

Brasserie Auval
397 Route des Pères
Val-d'Espoir, QC
G0C 3G0
auval.ca

Nanobrasserie Brett et Sauvage
37 Chemin de Saint-Isidore
Sainte-Thérèse-de-Gaspé, QC
G0C 3B0
brettetsauvage.com

WHERE TO TRY THIS BEER

Right on-site or, in the summer, on the brewery's patio, on rue de l'Anse.

WHERE TO BUY THIS BEER

At the factory shop annexed to the brewery (rue de l'Anse) and at several retail outlets throughout the province.

AMQUI

AT THE TOP OF THE THREE SISTERS

STARTING POINT	DESTINATION
DÉPÔT À SOUCY	DÉPÔT À SOUCY
BEER	**DIFFICULTY**
POINTE FINE	MODERATE
DOG FRIENDLY	**SEASON**
YES, ON LEASH	JUNE TO NOVEMBER
FEES	**DURATION**
NO	2.25 HOURS
MAP REFERENCE	**LENGTH**
AVAILABLE ON-SITE OR AT HIKE STARTING POINT	5.9 KM
HIGHLIGHTS	**ELEVATION CHANGE**
LAKE MATAPEDIA, THE THREE SISTERS	ASCENT: 150 M DESCENT: 150 M

EXOTIC IPA

YELLOW, CLOUDY

CITRUS, PINEAPPLE

CITRUS, PINEAPPLE, COCONUT, HOPS

BITTERNESS

SWEETNESS

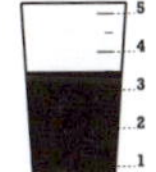

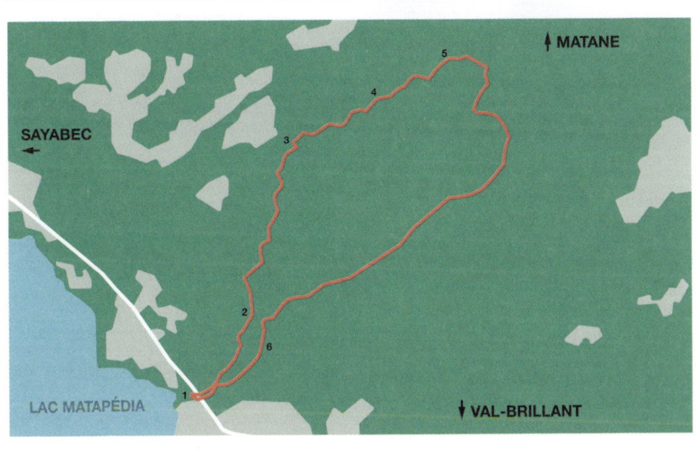

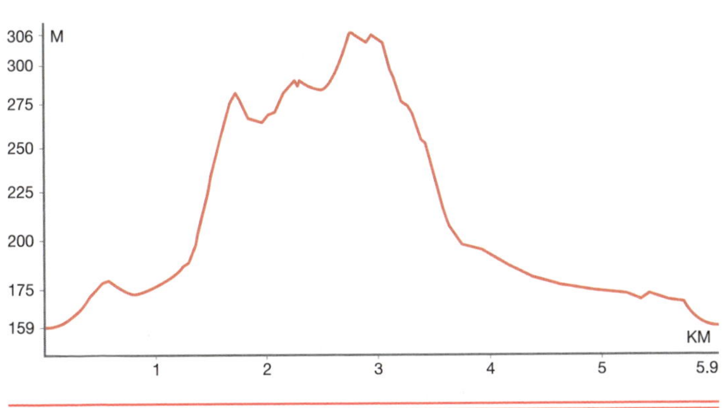

HIKE DESCRIPTION

Visit with The Three Sisters near Matapedia River and end your adventure in a former police station!

Amqui is part of the administrative region of Bas-Saint-Laurent, but from a tourism perspective, it's part of the Gaspé Peninsula. Occasionally, the town is mentioned in the context of both of these regions.

Parc régional de la Seigneurie-du-lac-Matapédia is situated in the valley and on the north shore of the lake of the same name. It also includes the towns of Amqui, Sayabec, and Val-Brillant. This forested area is both home and haven for a number of species: the black bear, the caribou, the bald eagle, the red fox, the ruffed grouse, and the snowshoe hare. The park boasts nearly 20 kilometers of walking trails ranging from easy to strenuous.

The Seigneurie-du-lac-Matapédia park is open from June to November. During hunting season, you are advised to wear an orange bib. Further, the park is home to native black bears and other creatures you might meet along the way. Giant hogweed has also been reported along the trail.

The trail named Les Trois Sœurs starts at the parking lot of Dépôt à Soucy[1] and takes you to three peaks over a distance of 5.9 kilometers. The peaks offer views of Lake Matapedia and a place that is home to numerous species of diverse animals. A part of the trail is shared with the International Appalachian Trail (IAT/SIA), and the last section, a trail called La Coulée, is shared with all-terrain vehicles (ATVs).

From the parking lot, cross the road and follow the signs that tell you to take the road on the right. The first part of the hike takes you through a relaxing, wooded area and over several little footbridges[2]. Keep your ears and eyes open: you might see some animal tracks in the damp earth. The trail is easy to follow and there's little chance of getting lost. That said, there are signs for Sentier Les Trois Sœurs along the way to remind you you're on the right path. If in doubt, look for IAT/SIA signs.

After a while, the land will rise gently and you will arrive at the first sister, a rocky summit[3]. Here you can see the Matapedia River. Resume your journey down, and then up again, higher than before. The second summit[4] (the second sister) has an observation deck that's just begging you to take a little break. It also has information on local wildlife.

Next, you're headed for the third sister[5], which involves another descent and another (and final) climb. There's a platform here, as well as a picnic table and outhouses.

It's already time to start heading back. Rejoin the trail where you left it before reaching the platform. After a short rise, you will gently start your way back down over a road that gets wider and wider. The last part of the trip follows an ATV trail on the right for about 2 kilometers[6].

When you're back at the car, return to the parking lot, to the left of the wooden pavilion. Go past the children's play area (next to the toilets) and treat yourself to a beautiful view of the lake and the beach (the sunsets are spectacular). Now you can return to your vehicle.

Take the road toward Amqui, where a warm welcome awaits you at La Captive, a microbrewery located in a former, century-old police station, which is now a local hangout. Order yourself a Pointe Fine.

Other options:
For a greater challenge, combine Les Trois Sœurs loop with Les Rochers, a 6.4 km trail (in and out) with the same starting point that runs along Lake Matapedia.

TRANSPORTATION

There is no public transit system servicing the park. The trailhead is located about 13 kilometers from the microbrewery, so a car is necessary.

From the town of Amqui, take Route 132 Ouest till you get to the covered bridge. After the bridge, take Rang Saint-Jean-Baptiste for about 250 meters before turning left onto rue Labrie. Keep going straight when you see the Pointe Fine sign. Dépôt à Soucy will be clearly marked.

TRAIL INFORMATION

Parc régional de la Seigneurie-du-lac-Matapédia
428 629-2053, extension 1035
lamatapedia.ca

TOURIST INFORMATION

Bureau d'accueil touristique d'Amqui (open June to September)
209 boulevard Saint-Benoît Ouest
Amqui, QC
G5J 2E9
418 629-5715

Tourisme Gaspésie
tourisme-gaspesie.com

LA CAPTIVE

Since 2010, La Captive in Amqui has occupied a space that used to be, at various points in time, a town hall, a fire station, a library, and a police station. Under new management since 2018, the brewery remains a local hotspot where Alexandre Pineau, proud brewer and co-owner, and his four sidekicks (all of whom met at the bar!) keep the place going strong. The bar's original stone arches and large garage door bear witness to the past and certainly add a certain charm. Indeed, some of the beer names are a throwback to all the things that used to go on there: l'Évadée (The Fugitive), l'Innocente (The Acquitted), la Coupable (The Guilty Party), la Traître (The Traitor).

BREWERY

La Captive
140 boulevard St-Benoît Ouest
Amqui, QC
G5J 2E8
418 631-1343
lacaptive.ca

WHERE TO TRY THIS BEER

Directly on-site.

WHERE TO BUY THIS BEER

Beers on the menu are sold in growlers.

GASPÉ

A BREATHTAKING VIEW OF LAND'S END

STARTING POINT	DESTINATION
CAP-BON-AMI PARKING LOT	CAP-BON-AMI PARKING LOT
BEER	**DIFFICULTY**
RIVIÈRE 'R' NORD	MODERATE
DOG FRIENDLY	**SEASON**
YES, ON LEASH	EARLY JUNE TO MID-OCTOBER
FEES	**DURATION**
YES, PARKS CANADA RATES APPLY	2.5 HOURS
MAP REFERENCE	**LENGTH**
AVAILABLE AT PARKS CANADA VISITOR CENTER	7.8 KM
HIGHLIGHTS	**ELEVATION CHANGE**
GULF OF ST. LAWRENCE, CAP-DES-ROSIERS LIGHTHOUSE, GASPÉ BAY, CAP-BON-AMI	ASCENT: 371 M DESCENT: 371 M

ENGLISH RED ALE

AMBER, DARK,
SEMI-CLOUDY

FLORAL AND FRUITY
HINTS, SUBTLE SPICES

MALT, TOASTED GRAIN

BITTERNESS

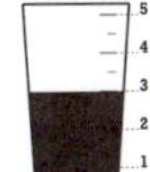

SWEETNESS

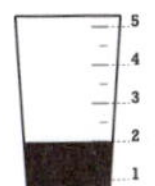

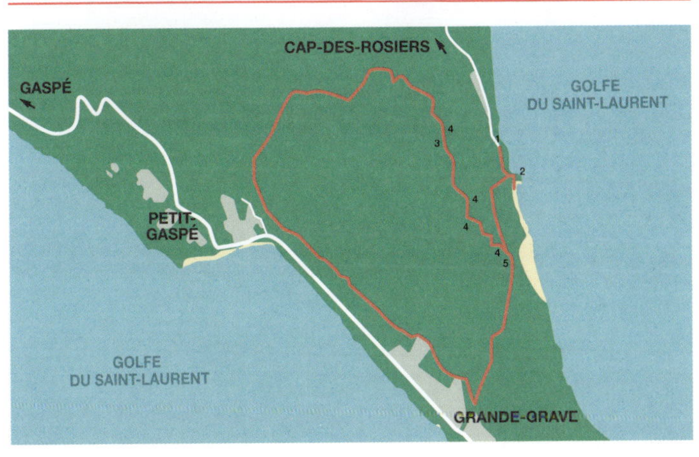

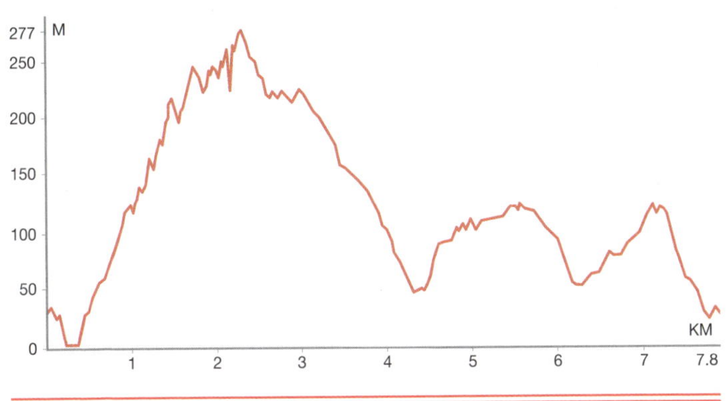

HIKE DESCRIPTION

Forillon National Park is 244 km² of unspoiled beauty. Located at the tip of the Gaspé Peninsula and tucked between the Gulf of St. Lawrence and Gaspé Bay, this park, managed by Parks Canada, offers 85 kilometers of marked trails, some of which are part of the International Appalachian Trail (IAT/SIA). How can anyone not be moved by its majestic landscapes made up of cliffs, capes, coves, crags, and coasts. People say that this peninsula is "the end of the world," and even the original inhabitants, the Mi'kmaq, referred to it as *Gespeg*, meaning "land's end."

The Mont Saint-Alban loop starts at Cap Bon-Ami in the north. If you're lucky, you might have a moose sighting (the animal's range is limited) or see seals basking in the sun (go to the side of the visitor center in Cap Bon-Ami parking lot and look down over the cliff).

The first thing you have to do is pay for your day pass at the booth at the north entrance, located along Chemin du Cap Bon-Ami. Here you'll also find the interpretation center, where you can get information on trail conditions and pick up a paper map. Make your way to the Cap Bon-Ami parking lot[1], where there is a building with toilets and drinking water.

The trail starts at the back of the parking lot but before heading there, first check out what's to your left: the Cap Bon-Ami lookout[2], which offers an impressive panoramic view. You've basically expended zero energy and already there's a painting before you! If you're in the mood, take the stairs down to the beach, go for a stroll, and enjoy a view that is more "down to earth."

Head back up, step off the lookout platform, and take a left. Sentier

Mont-Saint-Alban, which starts off quite steep, hugs the cliff and the trail quickly leads you to a set of stairs on the right. Now, you have two choices (it's a win-win situation and entirely up to you!):

1. Go up right away and reach the summit in less than 2 kilometers. If this is what you choose, the payoff is immediate but the cost is a very strenuous climb. With this more physically demanding option, the beautiful panoramic views[4] are front-loaded and the hike ends with a trail that is relatively easy and uneventful.

2. Go straight ahead and save the best for last.

Let's assume you chose the first option and are on the stairs to your right. For the next 1500 meters or so, the views become more and more interesting[4] (your reward) and as you climb, you'll come to the foot of the observation tower[3]. Take a deep breath and go up. At the top of the tower, a 360° view of beauty comes together in a single moment.

Before and all around you is the Gulf of St. Lawrence, the Cap-des-Rosiers lighthouse, the tip of Cap Gaspé, Cap Bon-Ami, Bonaventure Island, and Percé Rock (to see these from a different angle, check out the Percé hike).

Once you've regained control of your emotions, head back down to *terra firma* and take the trail to your right. This trail starts with a gradual descent (and there are stairs in some places) before quickly flattening out for a good spell. This section of the trail lacks notable views but instead offers charming undergrowth, a few animals here and there, little bridges spanning pretty streams, and a soothing atmosphere.

After about 5 km there will be intermittent openings in the trees that offer glimpses of the sea stretching out to the horizon. In no time, you will be at the bottom of the stairs[5] you climbed earlier and you will have completed the loop. Take the road back toward the parking lot, exit the park by Route 132 heading right, and make your way to Rivière-au-Renard and Au Frontibus microbrewery, where a good Rivière 'R' Nord red ale awaits.

Notes:
There are also hikes leaving from the entrance to L'Anse-aux-Griffons, closer to Rivière-au-Renard where Au Frontibus microbrewery is located. However, given Sentier Mont-Saint-Alban's dramatic character, opt for a hike with a starting point that is a little farther (a car is required in any case). If you're going to go so far east in the province, you might as well let your eyes get their fill!

Other options:
Like many, you could decide to simply turn back at the lookout, which is fine as you still get your money's worth!

For a completely different setting, there's the trail called Les Graves (15.5-kilometer round trip), which starts at Grande-Grave and has you hopping along coves toward the cliff and the famous "Land's End."

TRANSPORTATION

Forillon National Park is accessible by coach from certain towns and cities. Information is available from Orléans Express. A regional transit system also allows you to get there from Gaspé (contact the tourism office for more information). Or you can get to Forillon by taking Route 132, which basically loops around the park. There is free parking at Cap Bon-Ami.

TRAIL INFORMATION

Forillon National Park
1 800 773 8888
pc.gc.ca/forillon

TOURIST INFORMATION

Bureau d'accueil touristique de Gaspé
8 rue de la Marina
Gaspé, QC
G4X 3B1
418 368-6335
gaspepurplaisir.ca

Tourisme Gaspésie
tourisme-gaspesie.com

AU FRONTIBUS

Patrick Leblanc, brewer, and Lydia Martin Bérubé, graduate of administrative studies, were both born on the Gaspé Peninsula and made a choice to come back to the region when their first child was born. They teamed up with Laurie Boissonneault and Claudia Martin (Lydia's mom) to open Au Frontibus in 2017. Patrick draws inspiration from the wide, open spaces around him and always has Gaspé's untamed character front and center when he dreams up his recipes. Every sip of his British- and Belgian-inspired beer is a reminder of the Gaspé landscape, thanks to ingredients selected from the peninsula, its boreal forest, and other little regional touches.

BREWERY

Au Frontibus
41 rue du Banc
Rivière-au-Renard [Gaspé], QC
G4X 5E3
418 360-5153
aufrontibus.com

WHERE TO TRY THIS BEER

Right on-site.

WHERE TO BUY THIS BEER

From the brewery's on-site gift shop.

SAINTE-ANNE-DES-MONTS

CHIC-CHOC HEIGHTS AND MOUNT OLIVINE

STARTING POINT	DESTINATION
RUISSEAU-ISABELLE PARKING LOT	RUISSEAU-ISABELLE PARKING LOT
BEER	**DIFFICULTY**
LA TRIPEUSE DES BOIS	STRENUOUS
DOG FRIENDLY	**SEASON**
NO	YEAR-ROUND
FEES	**DURATION**
YES, SÉPAQ RATES APPLY	6 HOURS
MAP REFERENCE	**LENGTH**
AVAILABLE AT CENTRE DE DÉCOUVERTE ET DE SERVICES	14.5 KM
HIGHLIGHTS	**ELEVATION CHANGE**
MOUNT OLIVINE, VIEW OF MOUNT ALBERT, WATERFALLS, AND LAC DU DIABLE	ASCENT: 627 M DESCENT: 627 M

BELGIAN PALE ALE WITH HONEY AND THYME

GOLDEN, CLOUDY

HONEY, MALT, GRASSY HINTS

HONEY, HERBS

BITTERNESS SWEETNESS

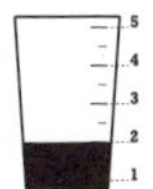

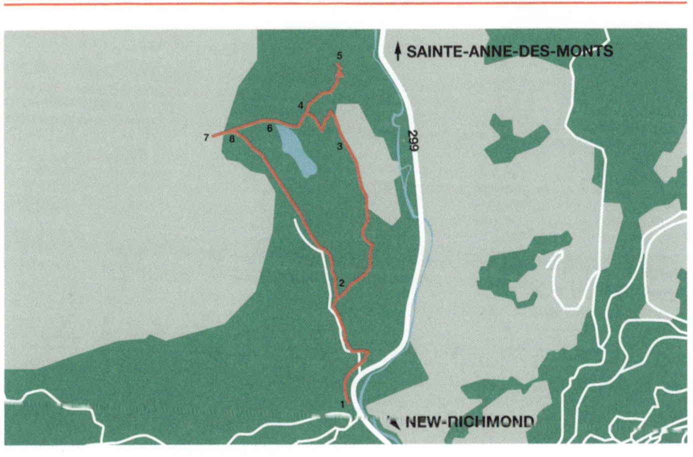

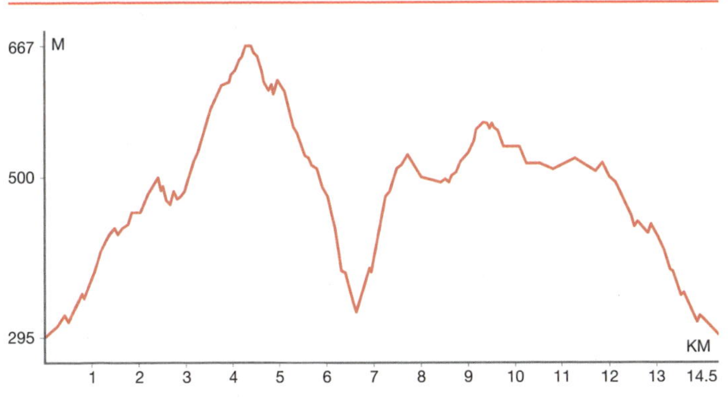

HIKE DESCRIPTION

Rise to the occasion in the Gaspé mountains and surround yourself with some of the highest peaks in Quebec.

The Parc national de la Gaspésie is a provincial park created in 1937 to protect the caribou herds, the salmon in the Albert River, and the beauty of the Albert and McGerrigle Mountains. The high-elevation summits, arctic alpine vegetation, and tundra landscapes make the park a stunning place where caribou still wander, the last enclave for this species south of the St. Lawrence River. Taking in parts of the Chic-Choc and McGerrigle Mountains, the park is renowned for the beauty and diversity of its hiking trails—short hikes ranging from easy to strenuous, and long-duration routes—and shares space with the International Appalachian Trail (IAT/SIA).

Ready to get high? This recommended hike takes you to the top of Mount Olivine and then sends you to a lookout with views of the Chute du Diable waterfall before wrapping up at the Abri de la Serpentine hiking shelter. The hike starts in the parking lot of Ruisseau Isabelle[1], a creek along Route 299. The Centre de découverte et de services, or Discovery and Service center, is located about 8 kilometers from there. Drop in for information on trail conditions and to pay your entry fee.

The journey starts with a steady but reasonable climb. The way is wide and easy and follows the hydroelectric pole line. About 1.8 kilometers in, you'll arrive at a clearing. The trail to Mount Olivine[2] is on your right. From here, the trail becomes narrower and gradually you'll find yourself in the woods and still climbing. The peak is 2.6 kilometers away and is preceded by incredible views and an enjoyable, well-marked trail.

After about an hour and fifteen minutes, you will be at the barren top of

Mount Olivine[3], at an altitude of 670 meters. Look around and you'll see a lake, Lac du Diable (you'll pass by it later), and majestic Mount Albert which, at 1151 meters, is one of the highest points in the Chic-Choc Mountains. Look down and you'll see how tiny Route 299 looks as it cuts through the park. To think you were there just an hour or so ago! Turn around and revel in the beauty of the path you took to get here.

You might catch a glimpse of a caribou from here, especially in the fall during the mating season (the trail that goes around Mount Albert is closed at that time). If you brought them, now is a good time to take out your binoculars!

Ready to leave? Seen enough? Well, it's not over yet! Keep going on this trail, which gets rockier and rockier. Go past the outcrop to start a somewhat demanding descent, which is nothing crazy...promise! Slowly but surely, you will make your way down. You will reach the point where the Grande Traversée and the IAT/SIA meet[4].

Here, head right and walk for a kilometer. Why? To get a view of Chute du Diable[5]. The trail is rather steep and there are lots of roots and stumps. The journey takes you down to an observation deck with views over the impressive waterfalls and you'll see ribbons of water shooting from mountainsides in the distance. Hike the one kilometer back.

Back at the trail intersection and the wooden footbridge, go straight toward Lac du Diable[6], which you'll hike next to for a while. Immerse yourself in the tranquility and think about how high you were just a short while ago.

With the lake behind you, another good climb awaits. You'll walk along a ridge where you can once again take in the 360° panoramic view and see Mount Albert and Mount Olivine (not to mention Lac du Diable and Ruisseau du Diable) under a new light.

Once you get to the Abri de la Serpentine[7] shelter, turn around, walk for a few minutes, and then take the trail in the direction of the parking lot[8]. This section of the trail takes you gently back to your point of departure but not without a few final glimpses of the striking mountains in the distance.

Back at the parking lot, take Route 299 toward Sainte-Anne-des-Monts (go north). Do what many of the park's hikers do and head for a microbrewery called Le Malbord. Here, you can celebrate your hard work and end the day on a high note.

Other options:
For the more adventurous hikers, and depending on the season, you could opt for the trail that loops around Mount Albert and start right from the Discovery and Service center. This hike is for experts and is about 17.8 kilometers.

If you're looking for an easier, shorter hike, the 4.5-kilometer, moderate-level Sentier Ernest-Laforce offers a good effort-to-reward balance. Make your way to the Mount Ernest-Laforce parking lot (Route 16) near the McGerrigle Mountains. From the discovery center, take Route 299 southward, followed by Route 16 on your left for about 7 kilometers. Follow the signs for Sentier Ernest-Laforce.

The Lac-aux-Américains Trail pairs well with Sentier Ernest-Laforce. It's an easy, short, linear trail ending with a cirque (a valley resembling an amphitheater and left behind by glacial erosion) that is beyond description. For a longer experience, head for Mount Xalibu, which begins just before the lake. Bear in mind that, unlike the recommended itinerary, some trails are closed part of the year, so check with the Discovery and Service center.

TRANSPORTATION

From Sainte-Anne-des-Monts (accessible via Route 132), drive for about 40 minutes along Route 299, southbound. Pay your entry fee and pick up a map of the trails from the Discovery and Service center. Then, make your way to the Ruisseau Isabelle parking lot.

The Sainte-Anne-des-Monts bus stop is located in the town center. There is a shuttle service between the Tourist Information center and the Discovery and Service center. Nonetheless, it's still easier to make your way around the park on your own (especially if you are not planning to set out from the reception area). Check with the tourist office or SÉPAQ for information.

TRAIL INFORMATION

Parc national de la Gaspésie
418 763-7494 or 1 800 665-6527
sepaq.com/pq/gas

The Discovery and Service center is open from mid-May to mid-October, and again from mid-December to mid-April. Self-payment options are available year-round.

TOURIST INFORMATION

Bureau d'accueil touristique de la Haute-Gaspésie
96 boulevard Ste-Anne Ouest
Sainte-Anne-des-Monts, QC
G4V 1R3
418 364-3544
vacanceshaute-gaspesie.com

Tourisme Gaspésie
tourisme-gaspesie.com

LE MALBORD

Thierry Lafargue began brewing at home in the 1990s. Even then, he had a passion for experimentation, as evident in his maple and birch sap beers. And why not? In 2014, Le Malbord's bistro opened, and finally the passion became profession when the microbrewery came along a year later. Thierry now makes his regional brews alongside Félix Labrecque, and outdoor enthusiasts coming down from the Chic-Choc Mountains have a place all their own to relax with a beer.

BREWERY

Le Malbord
178 1ére avenue Ouest
Sainte-Anne-des-Monts, QC
G4V 1C9
418 764-0022
lemalbord.com

WHERE TO TRY THIS BEER

Directly on-site.

WHERE TO BUY THIS BEER

Épicerie Thibault (specialty grocer)
88 rue Carignan
Sainte-Anne-des-Monts, QC
G4V 2M4

MAGDALEN ISLANDS

ÉTANG-DU-NORD

BETWEEN THE WIND AND THE TIDE

STARTING POINT	DESTINATION
CAFÉ-BISTRO LES ARAYNES (HAVRE-AUBERT)	MICROBRASSERIE À L'ABRI DE LA TEMPÊTE
BEER	**DIFFICULTY**
BOMBE DE SOLEIL	MODERATE
DOG FRIENDLY	**SEASON**
YES, ON LEASH	MID-MAY TO MID-OCTOBER
FEES	**DURATION**
NO	5 HOURS
MAP REFERENCE	**LENGTH**
AVAILABLE AT MAGDALEN ISLANDS VISITOR CENTER	18.5 KM
HIGHLIGHTS	**ELEVATION CHANGE**
HAVRE-AUBERT, BEACHES, BAIE DU PORTAGE, ÉTANG DU PORTAGE	ASCENT: 71 M DESCENT: 74 M

CITRUS DRY PALE ALE

GOLDEN, SUNNY

CITRUS, FRUIT, HOPS

CITRUS, DRY
AND FRUITY

BITTERNESS

SWEETNESS

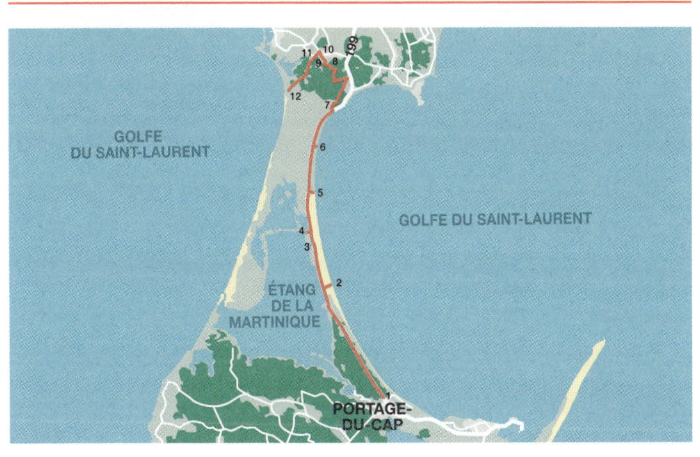

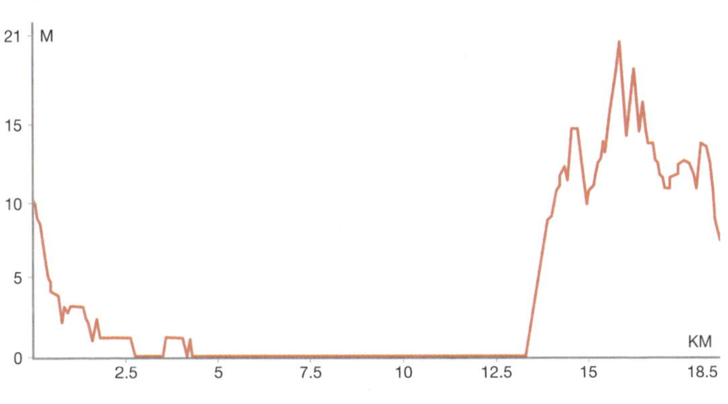

HIKE DESCRIPTION

There's no escaping the lure of the Magdalen Islands. Whether you dream of visiting, returning, or moving there—how nice would that be! —this place has an undeniable appeal that captivates anyone who sets foot there. Do a section of Sentier entre Vents and Marées (SEVEM), a trail network named for the ever-present winds and tides, and let the moment wash over you with every step you take.

Here on the islands, beauty is everywhere all at once, and the best way to explore it is definitely on foot. Even those from Magdalen Islands who have walked the Camino de Santiago think so. SEVEM opened in 2017 and comprises 230 kilometers of marked trails allowing hikers to discover the islands in 13 stages, each ranging from 10–28 kilometers.

Let's do the fourth stage of the mini-Camino, which starts at Havre-Aubert and ends at Étang-du-Nord. This hike will end at the microbrewery even though the trail continues for another 4 kilometers.

Get yourself to Les Araynes[1], a café/bistro on the island of Havre-Aubert. Facing Route 199, turn left. Apart from a few places that veer off to the left or right[2,4,5,6], the first 12 kilometers are pretty much a straight line. This allows you to stay on Route 199 for 12 kilometers, but you do have the option of taking a parallel trail[3] at roughly the halfway mark. If you're following the signage, you'll stay where you are, but if you prefer the earth over pavement, take the alternate path.

While you're at it, you might as well cross the road from time to time and venture out onto the two beaches: Plage du Cap and Plage de la Martinique. You can even opt to do a part of the trail with your feet in the sand by walking along the water's edge. You can hop back on Route 199 at any time, and the good news is that it's impossible to get lost.

After about 12 kilometers on the main trail, an arrow on the ground will tell you it's time to leave the pavement behind. Just beyond the observation deck[7] (on the other side of the trail, near a small, blue house), get on the ATV (all-terrain vehicle) trail and continue for about 3 kilometers. Make sure you follow the SEVEM signs, which are usually fairly easy to spot (yellow arrows, seashells, and the trail's logo).

You are now entering a wooded area. After passing a white building and turning left, you'll find yourself in front of a tower[8]. Go around it to the left, where the trail continues. About 500 meters later, you'll happen upon Chemin du Bois-Brûlé[9]. Take this road to the right. It turns into Chemin Chiasson[10] and here, there's asphalt underfoot once again.

At Chemin Coulombe[11], turn left and keep going for about 2 kilometers. Your microbrewery, À l'Abri de la Tempête (Sheltered from the Storm)[12], is at the end on your right.

Ready for that beer? Head inside and grab a table on the deck, order

a Bombe de Soleil (A Sun Bomb) and trip out on the unforgettable atmosphere that only the islands can offer.

Notes:
If you decide to do the entire SEVEM network, you'll have about two weeks' worth of hiking and you'll get to the microbrewery around the fourth day.

Other options:
Why not extend your adventure for no other reason than to check out Plage du Corfu (just keep following the signs for SEVEM)? When you're finished with this beach, head back and enjoy a gorgeous sunset from the deck.

TRANSPORTATION

You can reach the Magdalen Islands by plane or boat. Once there, you can use the public transit system, but the easiest option (assuming you didn't take your own car or bike aboard the ferry) is to rent a scooter or car (inquire at the rental agency on the islands).

TRAIL INFORMATION

Tourisme Îles-de-la-Madeleine

TOURIST INFORMATION

Tourisme Îles-de-la-Madeleine
Bureau d'information touristique
128 Chemin Principal
Cap-aux-Meules, QC
G4T 1C5
418 986-2245
tourismeilesdelamadeleine.com

À L'ABRI DE LA TEMPÊTE

Élise Cornellier Bernier and Anne-Marie Lachance met while studying art in Montreal. Élise was a brewmaster and had already been brewing professionally for a long time when Anne-Marie, with her entrepreneurial spirit, suggested they head off to the Magdalen Islands. It didn't take long for Élise, a kite enthusiast, to get on board with the idea. Partners in life and business, they had the crazy idea to open a microbrewery on the islands. With an old, abandoned building, a lot of grit and hard work, and a shared passion for the area and its inhabitants, their efforts have paid off. In 2004, their microbrewery turned its lights on and has been a checklist destination ever since.

BREWERY

À l'abri de la Tempête
285 Chemin Coulombe
L'Étang-du-Nord, QC
G4T 3V5
418 986-5005
alabridelatempete.com

WHERE TO TRY THIS BEER

Right from the microbrewery, which is open seven days a week during high season, but with restricted hours the remainder of the year.

WHERE TO BUY THIS BEER

At the microbrewery shop or in just about any grocery store on the islands.

LANAUDIÈRE

SAINT-DONAT-DE-MONTCALM

BLACK MOUNTAIN PEAK AND LIBERATOR LOOKOUT

STARTING POINT	DESTINATION
MONTAGNE NOIRE PARKING LOT	MONTAGNE NOIRE PARKING LOT
BEER	DIFFICULTY
ALFONSO	MODERATE
DOG FRIENDLY	SEASON
YES, ON LEASH	YEAR-ROUND
FEES	DURATION
NO	5 HOURS
MAP REFERENCE	LENGTH
AVAILABLE AT VISITOR CENTER	12 KM
HIGHLIGHTS	ELEVATION CHANGE
BLACK MOUNTAIN PEAK, ARCHAMBAULT LAKE, LE MÉSANGEAI REFUGE, SITE OF THE LIBERATOR AIRPLANE CRASH	ASCENT: 518 M DESCENT: 518 M

MANGO PALE ALE

YELLOW

MANGO, EXOTIC FRUIT

MANGO, HOPS

BITTERNESS

SWEETNESS

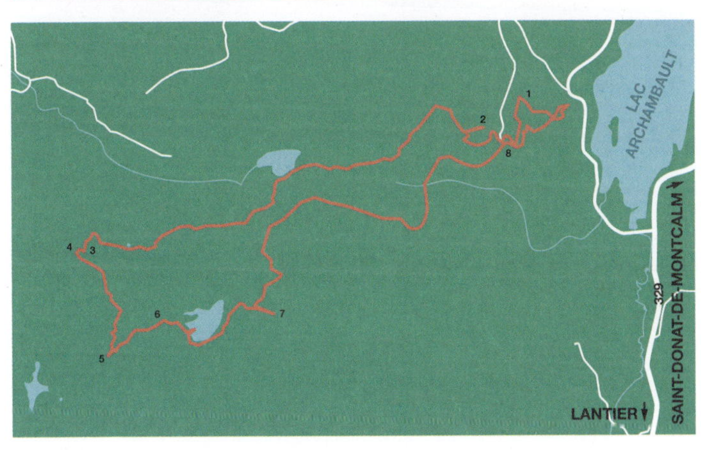

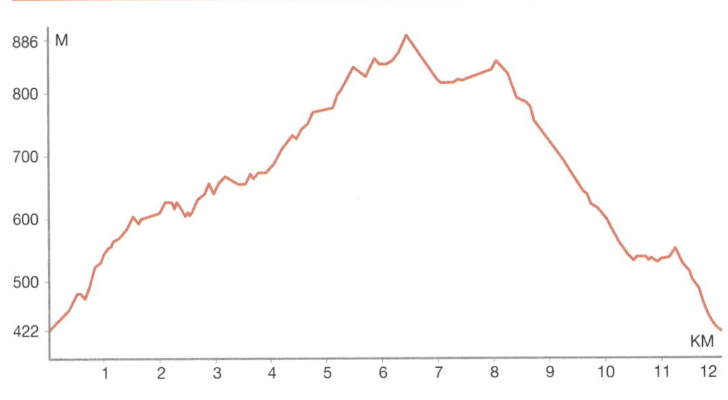

HIKE DESCRIPTION

The area around Saint-Donat-de-Montcalm, a small town in the regional county municipality of Matawinie, is renowned for its outdoor activities. It has a generous selection of walking trails, too!

The suggested activity for this region is the 892-meter hike to the top of Montagne Noire, or Black Mountain. The Belvédère du Liberator (Liberator Lookout) is along the way and there, you can see the remains of a plane that crashed in 1943. This moderate-level hike has no shortage of things to see!

The hike starts in the Montagne Noire parking lot, located on chemin Régimbald, about 8 kilometers from the microbrewery. A second parking lot is located a little before, along the same road. Both lead to the trailhead. The directions are focused on parking lot P1, where you will find outhouses and a sign with a map of the trails.

Your first trail is Sentier Inter-Centre[1], which was created more than 35 years ago and includes portions of the Lanaudière and Laurentian regions. The Lanaudière section is the one that will take you to the top of Black Mountain. For about 2.5 kilometers the trail is wide and barren and therefore rather easy, apart from the steady climb. This section is part of Quebec's Sentier National, or national trail. After you've walked for just a kilometer, you'll reach the first viewpoint[2], Archambault Lake.

About a kilometer later, the terrain gets rougher and slightly uneven. Just before the halfway point, not far from the peak, you'll find yourself staring at a most unusual sight: a plane crash[3]. On October 20, 1943, *Harry*, a Liberator III aircraft in the Royal Canadian Air Force, took off from Gander, Newfoundland en route to Mont-Joli Airport and was driven off course by bad weather. It never reached its destination hundreds of miles to the east. The plane collided with the mountain, taking the lives of all 24 souls aboard. It remains the deadliest plane crash in the history of Canadian military aviation.

Go past the first area of debris until you get to the cemetery[4], where you can observe a moment of silence. Then return and climb to the lookout, where the view is simply magnificent.

Resume your journey by following the signs to the top of Black Mountain, about a kilometer further. The trail will remain somewhat challenging, but it's well worth the effort. Promise! At the top of the mountain, climb the observation tower[5] and marvel at the breathtaking, 360° panoramic view of the Laurentian and Lanaudière mountains.

With your feet back on solid ground, go to the end of the open space at the foot of the tower and take Sentier de la Montagne Noire[6] until you get to a refuge named Le Mésangeai[7]. There, you're in for a lovely view of Crystal Lake.

Now take Sentier des Randonneurs[8] and eventually you'll find your way to the parking lot where you started (but pay attention to the signage to make sure you end up at the right one!).

Did you feast your eyes? Well, now it's time to treat your tastebuds! Hop back in your car and take Régimbald in the opposite direction. Turn left at Route 329, and then left again at Route 129 (which turns into rue

Principale). Keep driving until you get to the Brouemalt microbrewery in the heart of the quaint village of Saint-Donat-de-Montcalm.

Once there, try a refreshing Alfonso, a mango pale ale that is also the Brouemalt's inaugural beer!

TRANSPORTATION

The Saint-Donat-de-Montcalm bus terminal is located across from the visitor center, not far from the microbrewery. From there, you'll have to find your own way to and from the starting point, about 10 kilometers away.

TRAIL INFORMATION

Parcs régionaux MRC Matawinie
1 866 266-2730
parcsregionaux.org

TOURIST INFORMATION

Bureau d'accueil touristique de Saint-Donat (visitor center)
536 rue Principale
Saint-Donat, QC
J0T 2C0
1 888 783-6628

Tourisme Lanaudière
lanaudiere.ca

MICROBRASSERIE BROUEMALT

Mathieu Gibeault and Fannie Bessette were in the middle of a six-month trip to Asia with their children when they felt the need—rather, a strong and pressing urge—to open a microbrewery back home. Fannie, a sommelier, and Mathieu jumped into the project heart and soul! In fact, Mathieu was still in Sri Lanka when he registered for the Institut Brassicole du Québec, the province's training center for brewing and distilling. Back in Quebec, Mathieu, with no prior brewing experience, surrounded himself with talented brewers and completed his training. His efforts have paid off. The most notable thing you'll notice at Brouemalt is the team's warm, unpretentious nature and the place's family atmosphere.

BREWERY

Brouemalt
353 rue Principale
Saint-Donat, QC
J0T 2C0
819 424-3311
brouemalt.com

WHERE TO TRY THIS BEER

Directly on-site.

WHERE TO BUY THIS BEER

Brouemalt sells some of its beers for takeout in growlers and cans.

LAURENTIDES

MONT-TREMBLANT

THE LAURENTIAN MOUNTAINS IN ALL THEIR GLORY

STARTING POINT	DESTINATION
CENTRE D'ACTIVITÉS TREMBLANT (ACTIVITY CENTER)	MICROBRASSERIE LA DIABLE
BEER	**DIFFICULTY**
EXTRÊME ONCTION	STRENUOUS
DOG FRIENDLY	**SEASON**
YES, ON LEASH (SUMMER ONLY)	YEAR-ROUND
FEES	**DURATION**
NO	4.5 HOURS
MAP REFERENCE	**LENGTH**
AVAILABLE AT TRAILHEAD	11.5 KM
HIGHLIGHTS	**ELEVATION CHANGE**
OLD TREMBLANT, MOUNTAIN SUMMIT, 360° VIEW OF THE REGION	ASCENT: 636 M DESCENT: 656 M

TRAPPIST MONK-STYLE BELGIAN

AMBER, SEMI-CLOUDY

CARAMEL, SPICES

SOFT CARAMEL, FRUITY, SPICY

BITTERNESS

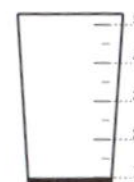

SWEETNESS

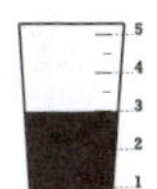

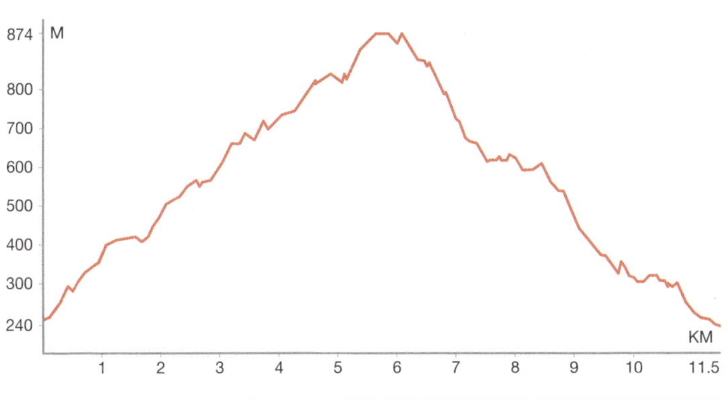

HIKE DESCRIPTION

Push yourself to the limit by scaling Mont-Tremblant, where the view of the Laurentian Mountains is spectacular. Finish off with Trappist-style beer that is certainly worthy of all your hard work. This hike is especially nice in the fall. The trails are closed when weather conditions are poor. Inquire before setting out. In winter, an alternate route may be necessary.

This 13 km hike starts at the foot of Mont-Tremblant[1], in the pedestrian village near Le Centre d'Activités Mont-Tremblant, or activity center. You can grab a paper map from the kiosk at your starting point.

Start your ascent by following the white and purple signs for Sentier des Ruisseaux[2]. Head slightly to the right where the climb is, at first, exposed. You will pass by a piece of land art by William "Bill" Vazan named *Réduire* (Reduce). Then follow the trail to enter the woods on your right.

You are still on Sentier des Ruisseaux. The path, easy to follow and well trodden, brings you along a small river, while nearby, clear water streams down rocky cliff faces. There are stairs here and there throughout this first part of the hike.

After a while, you'll come to Sentier Grand-Brûlé[3], with its white and red signs, and this is the path you'll follow to get to the top of the mountain. There are several viewpoints along the way. Some people find this trail somewhat challenging. Allow 2.5–3 hours to get to the top. You will pass through a deciduous area, a spruce forest, a marsh, and ski runs (where you'll be exposed to the sun but get pretty views and an idea of just how far you've gone). The ascent ends on a gravel road that leads to the station at the peak[4], an elevation of 875 meters. Take Sentier 360 and climb the observation tower[5]. Take a moment at the summit to enjoy the 360° view out over the Laurentians.

Ready to head back down? You can pay a few dollars and take the gondola back down (you'll be sweating), but honestly, it's much more satisfying to complete the loop by hiking your way back down. To do this, first go left to get to Sentier des Caps[6], where the white and green signage will be your guide for the next 5 kilometers or so. The good news is that the way down is not as steep as the way up. Alternatively, you can take Sentier Vertigo. Both trails run parallel to one another, and sometimes cross over, but both will take you to the foot of the mountain.

At the end of Sentier des Caps, get back on Sentier des Ruisseaux[7] (with its white and purple signage). It will split to give you two options: going left will send you in and out of the woods, across a ski slope, and reconnect you with the path on other side (where you began your climb); going right places you on a gravel road that winds downward around the mountain. The first option is the best, as it runs along a pretty river for a while and there are cascading waterfalls that will inspire you to push through the last kilometer.

Once back at your starting point, head straight for about 300 meters. La Diable[8], your microbrewery, is slightly off to the left. You'll find the Extrême Onction, a beer inspired by Trappist monks, to be well worth today's effort. Settle in on the patio, grab a food menu, and let Mont-Tremblant's village atmosphere soak in.

TRANSPORTATION

Public parking (for a fee) is available at the entrance to the pedestrian village. If you are arriving by coach, you'll be dropped off in another area. A free transit service connects the different areas to the resort where the hike starts. Inquire with Tourisme Mont-Tremblant.

TRAIL INFORMATION

Mont-Tremblant
tremblant.ca

TOURIST INFORMATION

Tourisme Mont-Tremblant
5080 Montée Ryan
Mont-Tremblant, QC
J8E 2W5
mont-tremblant.ca

Tourism Laurentians
laurentides.com

LA DIABLE

La Diable was the first microbrewery in the Hautes-Laurentides region. It's a story of passion shared by two engineers in search of new horizons. André Poirier and Pierre Jasmin toured the best brewpubs in eastern North America and then, in 1995, started out on their own. Ever since, they've been busy brewing little gems they love to share with visitors to Mont-Tremblant.

BREWERY

Microbrasserie La Diable
117 chemin Kandahar
Mont-Tremblant, QC
J8E 1B1
819 681-4546
microladiable.com

WHERE TO TRY THIS BEER

Directly on-site.

WHERE TO BUY THIS BEER

Directly on-site.

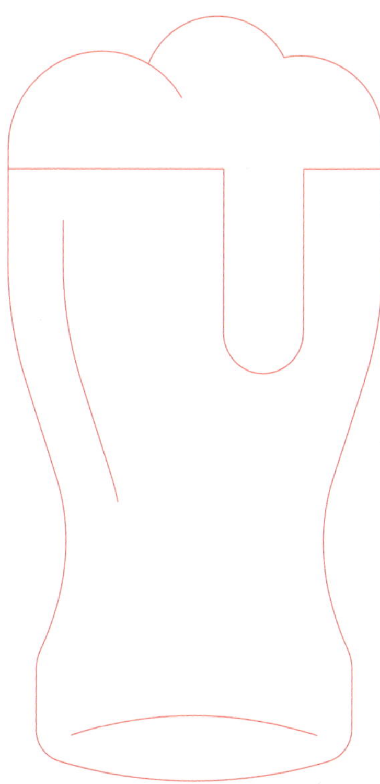

VAL-DAVID

ERRATIC BOULDERS, A VILLAGE ATMOSPHERE, AND A PINT OF AMBER

STARTING POINT	DESTINATION
CHALET ANNE-PICHÉ	AUBERGE-MICROBRASSERIE LE BARIL ROULANT
BEER	**DIFFICULTY**
QUEBEC PALE ALE	MODERATE
DOG FRIENDLY	**SEASON**
YES, ON LEASH	YEAR-ROUND
FEES	**DURATION**
YES	3.5 HOURS
MAP REFERENCE	**LENGTH**
AVAILABLE AT CHALET ANNE-PICHÉ RECEPTION	7.8 KM
HIGHLIGHTS	**ELEVATION CHANGE**
VILLAGE OF VAL-DAVID, ERRATIC BOULDERS, MOUNT CONDOR, MOUNT KING	ASCENT: 276 M DESCENT: 276 M

AMBER ALE

AMBER, SEMI-CLOUDY

CARAMEL, SPICES

FRUITY, CARAMELIZED, LIGHTLY SPICED

BITTERNESS

SWEETNESS

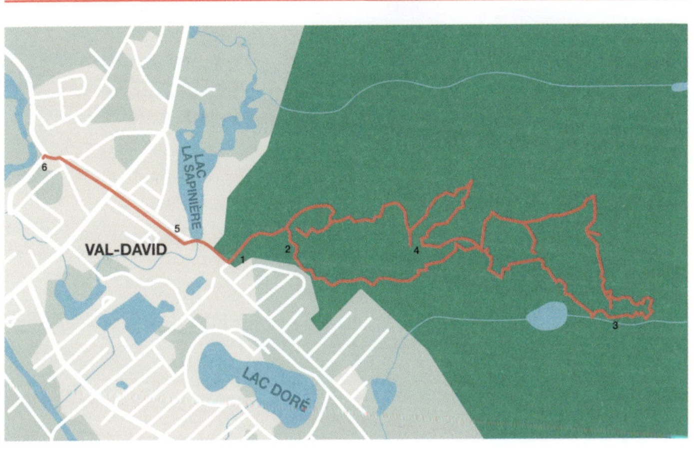

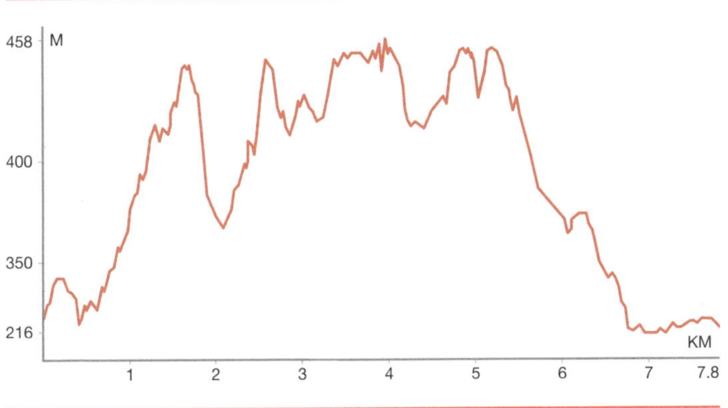

HIKE DESCRIPTION

Set out from a quaint village, stroll past rock fragments left in the wake of a passing glacier, admire cliffs coveted by rock climbers, and cap off your day with a pint of amber!

Here you are, in the charming village of Val-David, in the heart of the beautiful Laurentides region, where community spirit and creative drive are palpable. Today, your mission is to explore the nature reserve in Val-David—Val-Morin regional park. Its 60 kilometers of marked walking trails are embedded in a unique topography that offers numerous viewpoints, allowing you to take in the striking, natural environment around you.

The hike begins to the right of the Anne-Piché chalet[1]. First, follow the signs for Sentier D (snowshoe trail)[2]. This trail wastes no time bringing you to the woods and the first erratic boulders. These are the remnants of rocks, swept along by a glacier and left to sit there after it melted. You'll notice that some are massive—making rock climbers all the happier.

Keep an eye on the signage. At this point on the trail, it's easy to get carried away and lose your bearings. Take Sentier C. At the next fork, you have a choice: staying on Sentier C to head back, or pushing ahead on Sentier F on your right. The first option brings you back to your starting point via Mount Condor West, offers a few lookouts, and loops for about 1.5 hours.

The recommended option is Sentier F, because then you will pass by impressive rock faces, which are excellent for climbing, and get a chance to admire them from above. This leads to a series of gorgeous panoramas, which unfortunately come at a price—the trail is full of ups and downs.

If you've chosen to take Sentier F, make your way toward Mount King[3]. After passing the climbing wall (with a bit of luck, you might even see a few fearless climbers), take a right at the next two turn-offs on Sentier F and follow the directions toward the lookouts. When you get to them, take Sentier L on the left. Shortly after, follow the path to the lookout on Mount Condor East. You're now above what you were admiring earlier.

Head back the way you came. Follow the signs on Sentier L to the left in the direction of Mount Condor West[4]. Again, pay attention to the signs guiding you back to Chalet Anne-Piché, but don't pass up the chance to take in the views (which might result in going back and forth).

To wrap things up, follow the signs for Sentier E, and then take Sentier C. This is the last opportunity to admire the view, so go for it!

Once back at your starting point, head right as you leave the parking area. Cross the street, after the bridge, to get to the P'tit Train du Nord bike trail[5]. You will see a bit of the Val-David village.

At Chemin de la Rivière, head left. Auberge-Microbrasserie Le Baril Roulant (a brewery with an inn)[6] is located across from Parc des Amoureux (Lovers' Park) and along the edge of a river, Rivière du Nord. A Quebec Pale Ale awaits you. Make sure to ask for a food menu, too!

Notes:
This hike is especially awesome in the fall.

Other options:
There's no shortage of walking trails in the Val-David—Val-Morin regional park. If you are in the mood for a shorter or longer hike, visit the tourist office and design your own route.

TRANSPORTATION

It is possible to take a coach to Val-David from certain municipalities.

You can also park your car at Chalet Anne-Piché where the trails start. You might also wish to park in the heart of the village, halfway between the park and the microbrewery.

TRAIL INFORMATION

Le Parc régional de Val-David—Val-Morin
Chalet d'accueil Anne-Piché
1165 chemin du Condor
Val-David, QC
J0T 2N0
819 322-6999
parcregional.com/condition-des-sentiers

TOURIST INFORMATION

Bureau d'accueil touristique La Petite Gare
2525 rue de l'Église
Val-David, QC
J0T 2N0
819 324-5678, ext. 4235
valdavid.com/tourisme-bureau-daccueil-touristique

The Laurentians
laurentides.com

LE BARIL ROULANT

Le Baril Roulant (The Rolling Barrel) was established in 2012 by Sonia Grewal and Patrick Watson. The former has a background in the restaurant industry while the latter studied microbiology and chemistry. The two have a love for craft beer and their adopted village. The couple's approach is both ethical and inclusive, and their love of imaginative, regional cuisine has become a showcase for local products. This commitment shines through in all four parts of their business: the inn, the pub (Val-David and Tremblant), the restaurant, and the microbrewery. It's this diversity that inspires Patrick and his associate, David Vachon, to brew their little hoppy miracles.

BREWERY

Auberge-Microbrasserie Le Baril Roulant (pub, restaurant, and inn)
1430 rue de l'Académie
Val-David, QC
J0T 2N0
819 322-2280
barilroulant.com

WHERE TO TRY THIS BEER

At the inn, the pub, or in the microbrewery's restaurant.

WHERE TO BUY THIS BEER

Microbrasserie et Boutique Le Baril Roulant
1650 Route 117
Val-David, QC
J0T 2N0
819 322-2710

PRÉVOST

FROM HIGH UP ON THE PRÉVOST CLIFFS

STARTING POINT	DESTINATION
OLD PRÉVOST TRAIN STATION	SHAWBRIDGE—MICROBRASSERIE ET CHARCUTERIE
BEER	**DIFFICULTY**
IPA 117	MODERATE
DOG FRIENDLY	**SEASON**
NO	YEAR-ROUND
FEES	**DURATION**
NO	3.5 HOURS
MAP REFERENCE	**LENGTH**
AVAILABLE AT OLD PRÉVOST TRAIN STATION	7.8 KM
HIGHLIGHTS	**ELEVATION CHANGE**
PRÉVOST CLIFFS, OLD TRAIN STATION, LAKE PARADIS	ASCENT: 283 M DESCENT: 283 M

AMERICAN IPA

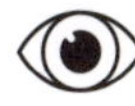

STRAW-YELLOW, CLOUDY

CITRUS, FLORAL AND GRASSY HINTS

CITRUS ZEST, HOPPY

BITTERNESS

SWEETNESS

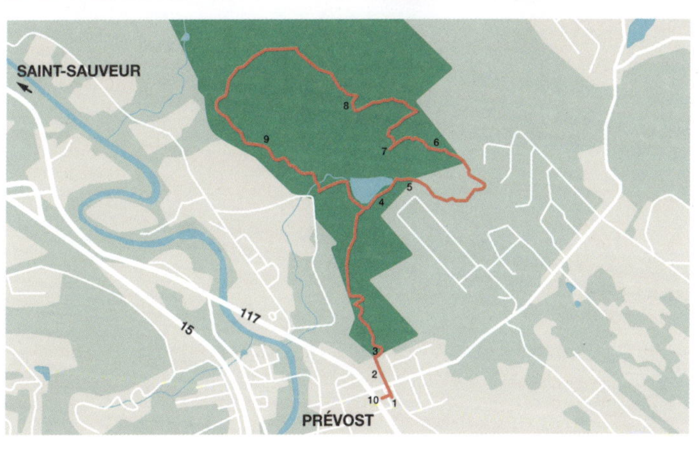

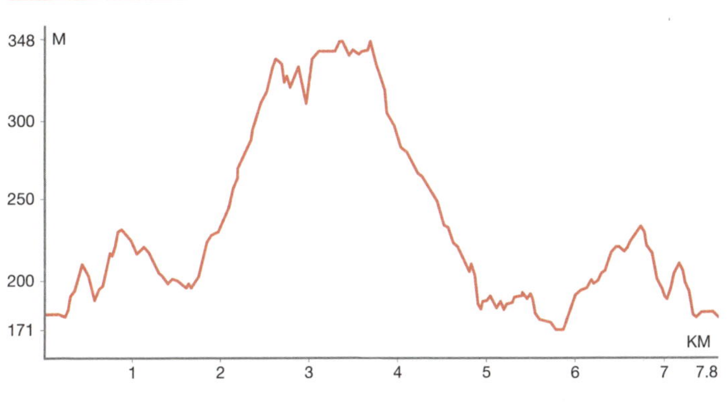

HIKE DESCRIPTION

From the P'tit Train du Nord to Prévost to Lake Paradis, there's no hike with a closer brewery at the end than this one!

The hike begins in front of the old Prévost train station[1]. From the parking lot, head for rue de la Station, cross at the crosswalk, and keep straight. You are on the P'tit Train du Nord[2] (Little Train of the North), the longest linear park in Canada and part of the Route verte (green route), a 230-kilometer former passenger rail line that once connected Mont-Laurier to Montreal but is now a multi-use trail and road system.

After just a few meters, you'll find the trail on your right, at the entrance to the Alfred-Kelly nature reserve. Named after a generous philanthropist, who was also a bird watcher and nature lover, the reserve is located smack-dab between Prévost's escarpments and Piedmont. It is protected by the Nature Conservancy of Canada.

Get on the first trail labeled MOC (McGill Outdoors Club—one of the oldest outdoor activity clubs in Montreal)[3]. After climbing the wooden stairs, turn left at the top and follow the signs. After a good uphill section, turn slightly right get to the Tour du lac trail[4]. At the next fork, go right and you will border the lake for a while.

At the end of the lake, take a right but instead of staying on the MOC[5] (slightly to your right), take Sentier de l'Escarpement[6], which will take you to a lookout atop the cliff. Be careful and respect your surroundings—this is a peregrine falcon nesting site and a protected reserve.

After the lookout[7], return onto Sentier de l'Escarpement, right where you left it. Then get back on the MOC trail on your left. After a while, you will start following the WN (Wizzard) signs[8], and then the JE signs[9], until you get to a fork where you will take a left back toward Tour du lac.

Facing the lake, go right and continue until you see the MOC trail again on your right. Take it. You have already been here, so just keep following the MOC signs until you get back to your departure point.

Once back on Le P'tit Train du Nord, go left. You will quickly notice a sign pointing the way to the microbrewery (that's service for you!). Keep going straight, cross the crosswalk, and head for the starting point in front of the old train station. Shawbridge—Microbrasserie et Charcuterie[10] is just behind it. You've definitely earned a nice IPA 117, a brew said to "go down much faster than the time it takes to get from Montreal to Abitibi." Why not grab some food, too? Perhaps sample some local products.

TRANSPORTATION

You can park your car in the parking lot at the old train station in Prévost.

TOURIST INFORMATION

Bureau d'information touristique des Laurentides
La-Porte-du-Nord rest stop
Exit 51, Autoroute des Laurentides
1 800 561-NORD (6673)
laurentides.com

SHAWBRIDGE – MICROBRASSERIE ET CHARCUTERIE

The Shawbridge microbrewery, also known as the Usine du Bon Vivant, is all sorts of good things rolled into one: good grub, quality products, terrific beer, a nice atmosphere, and friendly service. Hugues Néron, owner-operator, and Thierry Gautrin Molotchnikoff, brewmaster, along with their associates have every right to thump their chests for having created a place people want to go back to again and again. On the restaurant side, you can enjoy several beer-based recipes and dishes that feature local and regional ingredients. You can also find permanent and seasonal beers with tastes that reflect Thierry's considerable experience and his meticulous pursuit of the perfect, tastiest ingredients, handpicked and curated. At the P'tit Magasin shop, you can fill up on homemade cured meats, pastries, and local products.

BREWERY

Shawbridge – Microbrasserie et Charcuterie (Usine du Bon Vivant)
3023 boulevard du Curé-Labelle
Prévost, QC
J0R 1T0
450 224-1776
shawbridge.ca

WHERE TO TRY THIS BEER

At La Station, the restaurant portion of the establishment.

WHERE TO BUY THIS BEER

At the P'tit Magasin, the local-product shop annexed to the brewery.

MAURICIE

SAINT-ALEXIS-DES-MONTS

FROM AQUEDUCTS TO PINTS

STARTING POINT	DESTINATION
PARKING LOT ON RUE PELLERIN	PARKING LOT ON RUE PELLERIN
BEER	**DIFFICULTY**
ZESTE NOIR	EASY
DOG FRIENDLY	**SEASON**
YES, ON LEASH	YEAR-ROUND
FEES	**DURATION**
YES, PAY AT THE VISITOR CENTER	2 HOURS
MAP REFERENCE	**LENGTH**
AVAILABLE AT THE VISITOR CENTER	6.8 KM
HIGHLIGHTS	**ELEVATION CHANGE**
LAC DE L'AQUEDUC, VIEW OF SAINT-ALEXIS-DES-MONTS VILLAGE	ASCENT: 174 M DESCENT: 174 M

LEMON ZEST PORTER

BLACK

DARK CHOCOLATE, TOAST

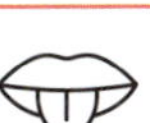

TOAST, COFFEE, CHOCOLATE, HINT OF LEMON ZEST

BITTERNESS

SWEETNESS

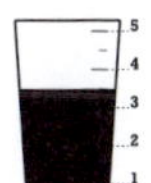

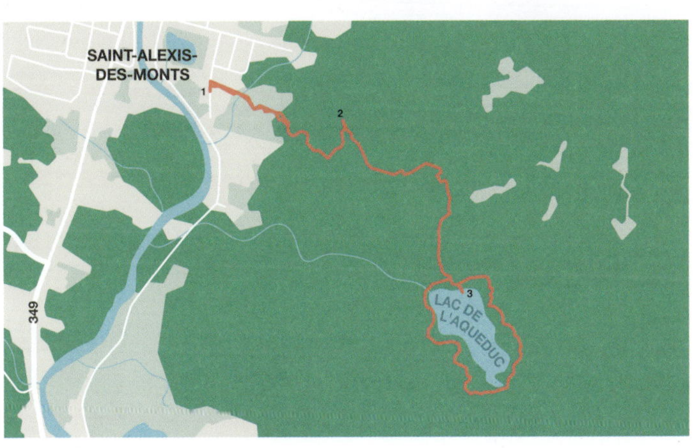

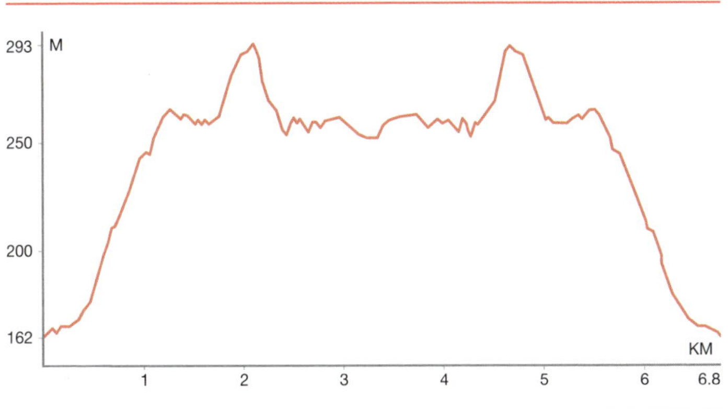

HIKE DESCRIPTION

Stroll along the bank of an old water supply at Lac de l'Aqueduc, fall in love with the charming village of Saint-Alexis-des-Monts, and then discover the Nouvelle France microbrewery. You won't regret it!

The village of Saint-Alexis-des-Monts is located in the county of Maskinongé, in the heart of the Mauricie region. With an area of 1153 km², it is one of the most spread-out municipalities in all of Quebec. It boasts 600 lakes and mixed forests and just oozes small-town charm. Time spent in Saint-Alexis-des-Monts is time well spent!

Today's hike on Sentier de l'Aqueduc is neither terribly long nor difficult but 100% enjoyable. It gradually goes deep into the woods, leads to a lookout and a gorgeous view of Saint-Alexis-des-Monts, and then dips down toward Lac de l'Aqueduc, which it deftly circumvents, before bringing you back to your starting point.

Begin the Sentier de l'Aqueduc trail from rue Pellerin[1]. The trail starts with a gentle rise until you get to a rocky promontory where a lookout[2], offering a view of the village and surrounding area, is located. After a short break, get back on the trail to the right of the promontory. The trail leading to Lac de l'Aqueduc, a haven of tranquility that once supplied the village with its drinking water, is well marked. There's a nice, short climb for those who appreciate a bit more of a challenge, but then the trail flattens out again. Once you are at the lake[3], the way around it is to your left, and that will take about 45 minutes. The path is narrow but well marked.

Other options:
To add a kilometer to your hike, you could also park in the village, near the visitor center, and walk to the starting point. If you also decide to walk to the microbrewery, that will add another 2.5 kilometers. In total, from the visitor center and back, you are in for an 11.8-kilometer adventure (from the hike to the microbrewery and back). Not bad at all!

TRANSPORTATION

You can park your car in the designated parking area on rue des Collèges. Or, you can also find parking in the village, near the visitor center.

TRAIL INFORMATION

La Nature d'Alexis
819 265-2015
lanaturedalexis.com

TOURIST INFORMATION

Accueil touristique de Saint-Alexis-des-Monts (visitor center)
10 rue Saint-Pierre
Saint-Alexis-des-Monts, QC
J0K 1V0
819 265-4110
saint-alexis-des-monts.ca

Outside the summer season, contact the municipality at 819 265-2046.

Tourisme Mauricie
tourismemauricie.com

NOUVELLE FRANCE

Nothing gets in the way of the family behind the Nouvelle France microbrewery. They're just bubbling with ideas and have an incredible ability to get things done. Marc and Martine established the brewery in 1998, but when Marc passed away, his sons François-Eugène and William took over the business. They decided to update the recipes and décor to suit their tastes and reflect their personalities. The result is this bold environment where Dave Lachance now brews his New France beers.

One thing that sets the owners apart is that, in 2000, they got into the business of making gluten-free beer. With support from Cœliaque Québec, a foundation dedicated to helping persons living with celiac disease, they became the first in North America to produce gluten-free beer from A to Z, from farm to bottle. In 2009, they acquired an agrotourism complex in Sainte-Angèle-de-Prémont, complete with a hop field, an orchard, a farmer's market, fields of amaranth, and much more! As you can see, there's no stopping this family.

BREWERY

Microbrasserie Nouvelle France
90 Rivière-aux-Écorces Road
Saint-Alexis-des-Monts, QC
J0K 1V0
819-265-4000
microbrasserienouvellefrance.com

WHERE TO TRY THIS BEER

Directly on-site, and check out the food menu, too!

WHERE TO BUY THIS BEER

This beer can be purchased on-site and in several retailers throughout Quebec.

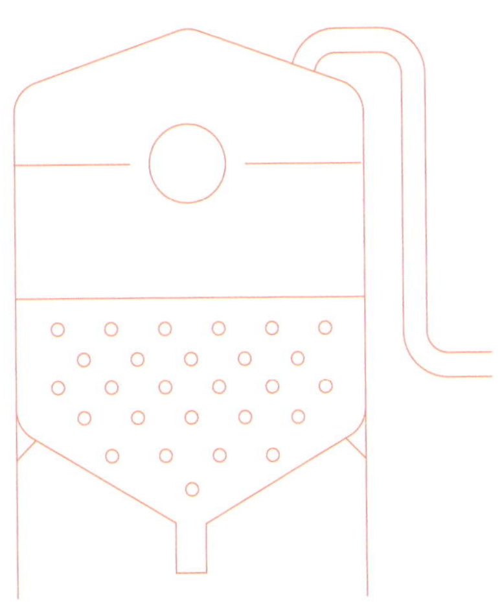

SAGUENAY—LAC-SAINT-JEAN

L'ANSE-SAINT-JEAN

A SPECTACULAR VIEW OF THE MAJESTIC SAGUENAY FJORD

STARTING POINT	DESTINATION
CHEMIN SAINT-THOMAS NORD	CHEMIN SAINT-THOMAS NORD
BEER	**DIFFICULTY**
LA PETITE CHASSE	STRENUOUS
DOG FRIENDLY	**SEASON**
NO	YEAR-ROUND (EXCEPT HUNTING SEASON)
FEES	**DURATION**
YES, SÉPAQ RATES APPLY	6 HOURS
MAP REFERENCE	**LENGTH**
AVAILABLE AT L'ANSE-DE-TABATIÈRE RECEPTION	13.5 KM
HIGHLIGHTS	**ELEVATION CHANGE**
VILLAGE OF L'ANSE-SAINT-JEAN, SAGUENAY FJORD, WATERFALLS, LAKE MORT, PEAK OF BLANCHE MOUNTAIN	ASCENT: 627 M DESCENT: 627 M

GRUIT

AMBER (ORANGEY EVEN), CLOUDY

FOREST, TEA, SPICES, WOODSY HINTS

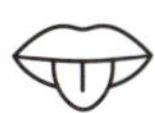

HERBAL, FIRRY, TEA, PEPPERY

BITTERNESS | SWEETNESS

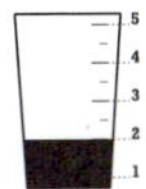

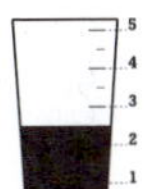

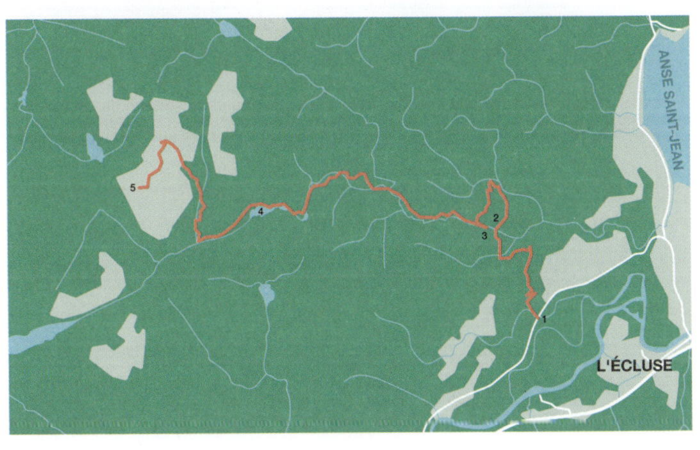

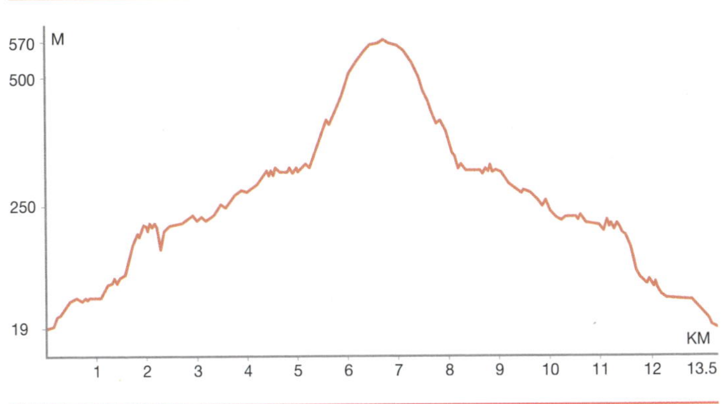

HIKE DESCRIPTION

The Parc national du Fjord-du-Saguenay, a provincial park named for the Saguenay fjord, straddles both shores of the glacier-carved fjord. It borders the Saguenay—St. Laurent Marine Park and three tourist regions: Saguenay—Lac-Saint Jean, Charlevoix, and Côte-Nord. The park boasts more than 100 km of hiking trails, and there's one spectacular view after another thanks to over 325 km^2 of natural beauty comprising coves, bays, mountains, and cliffs.

The hike takes place in L'Anse-Saint-Jean, in the area of L'Anse-de-Tabatière, and culminates at the park's most accessible peak Montagne Blanche, or Blanche Mountain (*blanche* meaning "white"), 565 meters above sea level. The vegetation is of the arctic-alpine variety, and the 360° view of the surrounding mountains and Saguenay fjord will blow you away!

The mountain's most striking feature is in the diversity of landscapes and terrains that you'll encounter as you hike 7 kilometers to the top. This hike is rated strenuous but can be completed by anyone with a good reserve of ambition. Allow 2 to 3 hours to get to the top and a little less to come back down.

The trail's start is well marked and is located on Chemin Saint-Thomas[1], where there is free parking. Consider paying your entry fee (cash only) at the self check-in or online before heading out.

The first part of the hike is actually another trail, Le Sentier de la Chute, and it takes you 2.5 kilometers to the first waterfall[2]. There, you'll link up with the trail that goes to the top of the mountain. Please note, Le Sentier de la Chute section is closed during moose hunting season. Check before heading out.

First, you'll meander through forest, over a well-marked and easy trail that leads to a maple grove. Enjoy the beautiful sights and sounds, and then head back.

Next, the trail narrows, dips back into the woods, and then zigzags up the side of the mountain as you continue your ascent. You'll quickly arrive at the foot of a waterfall—it alone makes the trip worth the effort! —and you might think it couldn't get any better, but keep going, as the best is still to come!

For the next few kilometers, keep going up. Cross through a mix of scenery that just keeps getting better. Eventually, there will be a sign

marking the start of the Montagne Blanche Trail, on the right. Before that, in front of you, you'll see a small, wooden bridge. Cross it and turn left to get a good view[3] of the charming village of L'Anse-Saint-Jean and the Saguenay fjord. Afterward, head back the same way (cross back over the bridge) and follow the signage toward the mountain.

The trail will be flat for a while and follows a brook before coming to a clearing. As you leave the woods, there'll be a wooden platform, which you'll cross before crossing the clearing. Continue along this relatively easy trail and enjoy it while you can, because soon it will get a little harder! Once again, you'll see intermittent waterfalls, erratic boulders, streams, lakes[4], and other bodies of water… all impressive visual hints of what's to come.

Once you get to Lac Mort (Dead Lake), follow the rocky trail around it. From this point, the degree of difficulty slowly and steadily increases. Take your time, you'll get there! The last two kilometers, which require hiking over steep wooden stairs and rocky promontories, offer a series of stunning views of the neighboring mountains and Saguenay fjord. The summit[5] of the mountain is devoid of vegetation, but it's where you've earned the right to gush over the views of the Saguenay fjord and mountainous scenery. Follow the yellow marks on the ground for guidance as you proudly swagger about. To get back down, simply retrace your steps and live the experience in reverse.

With the hike over, head for the village and Bistro de l'Anse for a good Gruit at La Chasse-Pinte cooperative brewery.

Other options:
For those who prefer a trail that is not so demanding, the moderate-level Le Sentier de la Chute, 5 kilometers in and out, is well worth your while.

TRANSPORTATION

If you find yourself in L'Anse-Saint-Jean, chances are you got there on your own (there's no official public transport). You can park your car in the village and walk to the starting point for the hike. Or you can just drive to the trail and park along the road.

TRAIL INFORMATION

Parc national Fjord-du-Saguenay
L'Anse-de-Tabatière reception area (closed from early November to middle of May)
418 272-1556
sepaq.com/pq/sag

TOURIST INFORMATION

Tourisme L'Anse-Saint-Jean
418 272-2633
tourisme.lanse-saint-jean.ca

Tourisme Saguenay–Lac-Saint-Jean
saguenaylacsaintjean.ca

LA CHASSE-PINTE

La Chasse-Pinte cooperative brewery is a venture—a project of the heart that took nearly a decade to come to fruition—started by a group of citizens who wanted to celebrate the riches of the boreal forest. In the Saguenay dialect of French, *chasse-pinte* refers to the cooking pot used for making *tourtière*, a traditional French-Canadian meat pie. After first acquiring the Bistro de l'Anse in 2013, the cooperative bought the old fire station in 2015 for the brewery. And that's where brewmaster Mathieu Boily now concocts his bold organic brews. The brewery has made its name by using native plants and, especially, malt and hops that are organically grown in Quebec.

BREWERY

Microbrasserie coopérative La Chasse-Pinte
220 rue Saint-Jean-Baptiste
L'Anse-Saint-Jean, QC
G0V 1J0
418 608-8559
chasse-pinte.com

WHERE TO TRY THIS BEER

Au Bistro de l'Anse (open from May to October)
319 rue Saint-Jean-Baptiste
L'Anse-Saint-Jean, QC
G0V 1J0
418 272-4222

WHERE TO BUY THIS BEER

Épicerie Amyro – Marché Richelieu, located right across from the microbrewery.

SAINT-FULGENCE

HIKE THROUGH THE WOODS, DRINK THE FOREST

STARTING POINT	DESTINATION
CENTRE DE DÉCOUVERTE ET DE SERVICES	CENTRE DE DÉCOUVERTE ET DE SERVICES
BEER	**DIFFICULTY**
LA FORESTIÈRE	STRENUOUS
DOG FRIENDLY	**SEASON**
YES, ON LEASH	YEAR-ROUND (WINTER: SNOWSHOE ONLY)
FEES	**DURATION**
YES, SÉPAQ RATES APPLY	3 HOURS
MAP REFERENCE	**LENGTH**
AVAILABLE AT THE CENTRE DE DÉCOUVERTE ET DE SERVICES	8 KM
HIGHLIGHTS	**ELEVATION CHANGE**
VIEW OF THE SAGUENAY RIVER, PIC-DE-LA-TÊTE-DE-CHIEN, VALIN RIVER	ASCENT: 352 M DESCENT: 352 M

BOREAL-SPICED AMBER ALE

GOLDEN, SLIGHTLY CLOUDY

CONIFERS, SUBTLE SPICES

WOODSY, HINTS OF TEA, SPRUCE

BITTERNESS

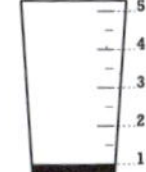

SWEETNESS

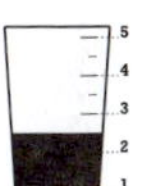

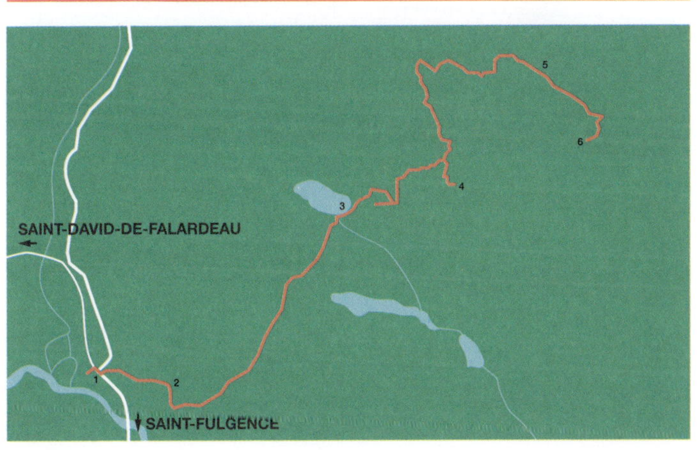

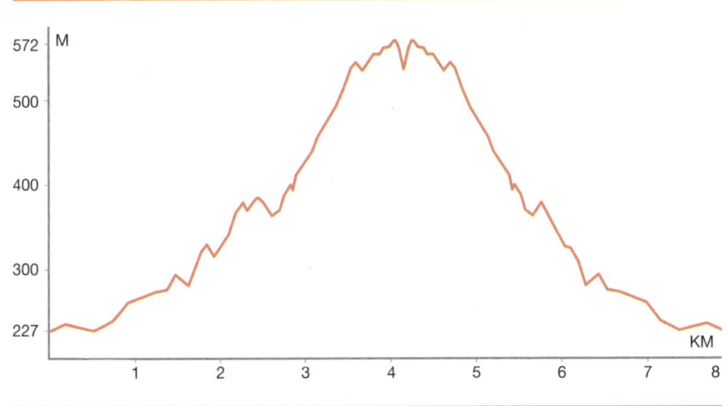

HIKE DESCRIPTION

Quebec's 154 km² Parc national des Monts-Valin, or Monts-Valin provincial park, is dominated by the region's highest peak: the 980-meter-high Mount Valin. The park has numerous trails on offer outside the cold season, but it's the magical Vallée des fantômes (Ghost Valley) that really gives this place its reputation. Nonetheless, the park has lots of wonderful things to see any time of year.

The Pic-de-la-Tête-de-Chien Trail will lead you to several vantage points and lookouts, including a rocky bluff where you can look out over some of the Saguenay region and see lakes, a peat marsh, and the Valin River.

The hike starts across from the park's Centre de découverte et de services[1] (Discovery and Visitors Center), reachable from the village Saint-Fulgence via Rang Saint-Louis, a distance of 17 kilometers. That's where you'll pay your SÉPAQ fees, fill your water bottle, and find information about the trail.

You'll find the directions as easy as following the signs toward Pic-de-la-Tête-de-Chien on the way out and following the signs pointing toward the reception on the way back.

Your first mission is to follow Sentier des Pics[2] over a wide, relatively flat dirt road that gently rises toward Lac des Pères[3], a lake you'll stay close to after taking a wooden footbridge. You might see a beaver dam or two. The lake is located at the foot of the mountain you will climb (the fun is just getting started). You'll cross a marsh before beginning your ascent up a steep trail that can be muddy and is dotted with exposed rocks and tree roots.

There are two spots where you can turn off to get a good view[4]. If you're in the mood, go for it. Alternatively, you can always wait for the views at the top if you want to save your energy, or you can check out the views on the way back down.

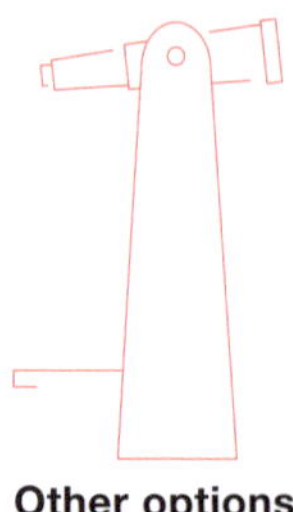

Eventually, you'll have a trail decision to make. Take the one marked Pic-de-la-Tête-de-Chien[5]. Along the way, several rocky paths will take you from one lookout to another, until you reach your destination[6] at an altitude of 570 meters. Once there, gaze out over the region. On a clear day, you can even make out the Saguenay fjord in the distance.

Other options:
If you're in the mood for a bigger challenge, head all the way to Pic-du-Grand-Corbeau (a 12-kilometer return) or Pic-de-la Hutte (a 16-kilometer hike in and out). Please be advised that dogs are only permitted on the Pic-de-la-Tête-de-Chien trail.

TRANSPORTATION

There is a bus stop in the center of the village, but there aren't many public transportation options to Saint-Fulgence. You'll also need to get to where the trails start, almost 20 kilometers beyond that.

If you are traveling by car, from the village, take rue du Saguenay westward, then Rang Saint-Louis toward the north for about 17 kilometers. You can park your car at the Discovery and Visitors Centre.

TRAIL INFORMATION

Parc national des Monts-Valin (Discovery and Visitors Center)
360 Rang Saint-Louis
Saint-Fulgence, QC
G0V 1S0
418 674-1200
sepaq.com/pq/mva

TOURIST INFORMATION

Tourisme Saguenay–Lac-Saint-Jean
1 877 253-8387
saguenaylacsaintjean.ca

LE SAINT-FÛT

Le Saint-Fût (The Holy Keg), a microbrewery that operates as a cooperative, is the result of four people who are passionate about beer: Maxime, Charles, Mélissa, and Jimmy. Their goal is to create quality jobs in a place—their beloved Saguenay—where opportunities do not necessarily abound. Le Saint-Fût and its three co-brewers have been making beer since 2018. The plants used to flavor them are handpicked by a local company in an environmentally sustainable way. What's more, most of the hops and malts used are grown in Quebec.

BREWERY

Le Saint-Fût
253-A rue du Saguenay
Saint-Fulgence, QC
G0V 1S0
lesaintfut.com

WHERE TO TRY THIS BEER

On-site, on the patio from May to September.

WHERE TO BUY THIS BEER

At the on-site shop (opening times vary by time of year, so check ahead). All corner stores in Saint-Fulgence, and several retailers throughout Quebec, sell beers from Le Saint-Fût.

GLOSSARY

As you hike and taste your way through Quebec, you'll no doubt come across a number of geographic and other terms on signs, maps, and interpretative panels (as well as in this book). The following is a list of French terms and their English equivalents that might just come in handy.

Anse
cove
Baie
bay (also berry!)
Belvédère
lookout
Bois
woods
Brasserie
brewery
Chemin
road
Chute(s)
waterfall(s)
Droite
right
Édifice
building
Église
church
Est
east
Étang
pond
Falaise
cliff
Fleuve
river (one that empties into the sea and has an estuary, and is therefore often of considerable size, just like the Fleuve Saint-Laurent, or St. Lawrence River)
Forêt
forest
Gauche
left
Halte routière
rest stop
Hôtel de ville
townhall or city hall
Île
island
Jardin
garden
Lac
lake
Métro
subway
Microbrasserie
microbrewery
Mont
mount
Montagne
mountain
Municipalité régionale de comté (MRC)
regional county municipality (RCM)
Nord
north
Ouest
west
Parc
park
Passerelle
footbridge
Phare
lighthouse
Place
square (in a town or city)
Pont
bridge
Promenade
boardwalk (by foot), drive (by car)
Randonnée
hike
Rivière
river (water flowing from one body of water [lake, river] into another [lake, river])
RTC
Réseau de transport de la Capitale (Quebec City's municipal transportation network)

Rue
street
Ruisseau
stream, creek, brook
Sentier
trail, path
Société des établissements de plein air du Québec (SÉPAQ)
provincial organization overseeing outdoor activity and establishments)
Sortie
exit
Stationnement
parking lot
Sud
south
Val/vallée
valley
Ville
town or city

TOP 5

MY 5 FAVORITE MICROBREWERIES
(in this book)

LE NOCTEM, Quebec City (Quebec City and Surrounding Area)

BREWSKEY, Old Montreal and the Old Port (Montreal)

À L'ABRI DE LA TEMPÊTE, L'Étang-du-Nord (Magdalen Islands)

LA GRANGE PARDUE, Ham-Sud and Ham-Nord (Eastern Townships)

TÊTE D'ALLUMETTE, Saint-André-de-Kamouraska (Bas-Saint-Laurent)

MY 5 FAVORITE HIKES
(in this book)

BLANCHE MOUNTAIN, L'Anse-Saint-Jean (Saguenay–Lac-Saint-Jean)

MOUNT HAM, Ham-Sud and Ham-Nord (Eastern Townships)

KÉKÉKO HILLS, Rouyn-Noranda (Abitibi-Témiscamingue)

MOUNT OLIVINE, Sainte-Anne-des-Monts (Gaspé Peninsula)

NOIRE MOUNTAIN, Saint-Donat-de-Montcalm (Lanaudière)

THIS BOOK IN NUMBERS

MONTHS TRAVELING QUEBEC'S ROADS

TOURIST REGIONS VISITED

4

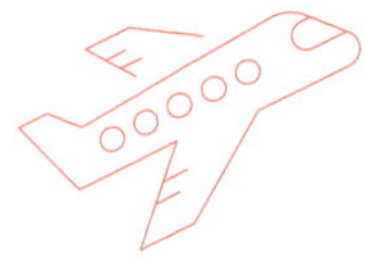

FLIGHTS FLOWN

20,015

KILOMETERS DRIVEN

484

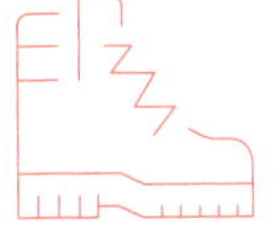

KILOMETERS WALKED

403

DIFFERENT BEERS TASTED

54

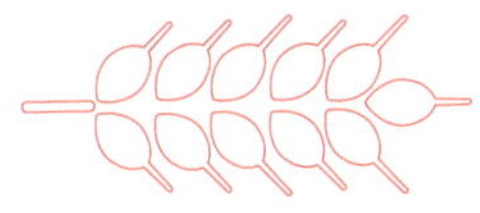

MICROBREWERIES VISITED (BUT MORE THAN 80 SCOUTED)

ACKNOWLEDGEMENTS

Just because there's only one name on the cover doesn't mean this book was a solo project. The "I" is actually a "we" and it includes those wonderful humans who helped me hike the trails or taste the beers (and sometimes both!).

I would especially like to thank my hiking pals: the father of my children, Simon, and my little big adventurers Maëva, Nora and Loïc; as well as Clément and Marilyn, Caro, Anne, Sam (samuelcyr.com), Annabelle (matanteA.com), Gabrielle (vagabondeuse.ca), Audrey (arpenterlechemin.com), Andréanne, Sandra, Karine, Josée and Christine. A special shout-out to Elliot, Milan, Lilyanne and Charles-Édouard, who kept my children company from time to time and, for their young age, racked up a good number of miles, too.

A special thank you to two brewers, Philippe Lord (Le Prospecteur) and Philippe Morin (La Panacée Brewing Co.), for their help. I can't forget my "personal beer advisors," faithful tap-take-over partners, and forever-friends: Héli and Dan. A big thank you also goes to Marie-Pier (Hoppy Mary) and David M. for their assistance with the Montreal hikes, and to Maude (MC Globetrotteuse) for her help in Quebec City.

I would also like to acknowledge the entire team at Helvetiq for their enthusiasm. Hadi, thanks for your faith in me. A special thanks to Chloé, my patient editor, for her always-valid comments.

I can't forget to say thank you to all the people who answered my endless questions (sometimes without even knowing I was working on the little wonder that is this book), all the brewers mentioned in these pages or their representatives, and the people in charge of the trails or the tourism offices, among others.

Thanks to photographers Samuel Cyr, Philippe Lord, Karine Murphy, and Eve Pouliot.

Finally, I have to thank all those who made my life a lot easier by giving me a place to roost for a night (Sandra D., Jessica and Philippe, Sam, Andréanne M., and Josée), as well as all the families who lent me their houses while they were away so I could take my family and explore the different regions (Andréanne D., Mélanie, Marianne, Chrystel and Charles, Sandra P., and their respective families).